Endorsements and Praise for Friend of God

Friend of God will help you fall in love with God all over again. It is one of the best books I have ever read. I highly recommend that everyone picks up a copy and reads it.

- **John E. Randell, Senior Pastor, Revive Church, OK**

My wife and I are thankful for the prudence and zeal put forth by Stony Kalango in writing *Friend of God*. We believe that these pages will provoke greater levels of hunger and thirst for righteousness in the hearts of believers across the globe. Our prayer is that the Lord would use this book to inspire a new generation of disciples of Christ to seek first the kingdom just as He did with *God Chasers* by Tommy Tenney and *Good Morning Holy Spirit* by Benny Hinn.

– **Joshua and Eliza Trent, Founders of Iron Scepter Worldwide and Senior Pastors of Freedom Church.**

Thanks be to God. This book, *Friend of God* has been written with the glory and anointing of the great Holy Spirit and I am blessed by it.

- **Rev Dr. Bishop Joseph Masih, Lahore, Pakistan.**

Friend of God

Discover Divine Friendship As You Become One After God's Own Heart

STONY KALANGO

Unless otherwise indicated, all other Scripture quotations are taken from the New King James Version by Thomas Nelson. Scripture quotations marked (NLT) are from the New Living Translation. Scripture quotations marked (ESV) are from the English Standard Version. Scripture quotations marked (CEV) are from the Contemporary English Version. Scripture quotations marked (MSG) are from the New Living Translation. Scripture quotations marked (NOG) are from the Names of God translation. Scripture quotations marked (AMP) are from the Amplified Bible. Scripture quotations marked (CSB) are from the Christian Standard Bible. Scripture quotations marked (NIV) are from the New International Version. Scripture quotations marked (EHV) are from the Evangelical Heritage Version. Scripture quotations marked (MEV) are from the Modern English Version. All rights reserved.

Friend of God: Discover Divine Friendship As You Become One After God's Own Heart.

Copyright © 2024 by Stony Kalango.

All rights reserved. No part of this publication may be reproduced, distributed, or transmitted in any form or by any means, including photocopying, recording, or other electronic or mechanical methods, without the prior written permission of the publisher, except in the case of brief quotations embodied in critical reviews and certain other noncommercial uses permitted by copyright law.

ISBN: 979-8-89587-078-5 (Paperback)

ISBN: 979-8-89587-082-2 (Hardcover)

First printing edition 2024.

www.stonykalango.com

DEDICATION

To my dear Olivia. She is indeed the melody that makes my life's symphony harmonious. She is the epitome of grace, elegance and resilience; a steady anchor with her unwavering love and support. She truly makes my life better.

And

To our two beautiful daughters, Honor and Hadassah. Their eyes and smile radiate boundless love, joy, wonder and hope. They are indeed a heritage from the Lord.

Contents

Foreword 1

Introduction 2

Chapter 1: God's Friends Love Him So Dearly 6

Chapter 2: God's Friends Have An Indestructible Trust In The Lord. 18

Chapter 3: God's Friends Walk In The Fear Of The Lord 28

Chapter 4: God Is Pleased With His Friends 45

Chapter 5: God's Friends Are Friends Of Other Believers 53

Chapter 6: God's Friends Are Not Ashamed Of God 63

Chapter 7: God's Friends Are Not Friends Of The World 70

Chapter 8: A Friend Of God Walks With God 78

Chapter 9: God's Friends Love His Presence 87

Chapter 10: God's Friends Speak To God, And They Listen To God 100

Chapter 11: God's Friends Lay Down Their Lives For God 120

Chapter 12: Friendship With God Is Only Through Jesus Christ 129

Chapter 13: God's Friends Love Others 135

Chapter 14: God's Friends Obey God 139

Chapter 15: God's Friends Are Passionate About God's Kingdom And The Gospel 148

Epilogue 169

Notes 171

About The Author 178

Foreword

It is a great honor to introduce you to Stony Kalango and Stony Kalango Ministries. I have been blessed the last several years to have Stony work alongside me as my Associate Pastor. Stony is an outstanding teacher/preacher. He teaches each Wednesday night with the dynamics of a powerful evangelistic teacher. I have been honored to call Stony and Olivia my friends. My wife, Joaneta, recently asked me what I thought of Stony's book, *Friend of God*, and I said, "It is one of the best books I have ever read."

I recommend it to young preachers as a study guide and as a source of inspiration for preaching. I also recommend it to seasoned preachers as a devotional book that will bring you closer to Christ and bring old truths to light again.

Stony has written 15 chapters, each one is powerfully anointed with great insight. In his first chapter, *God's Friends Love Him Dearly*, he quickly captivates your attention with a list of 68 statements explaining why he loves the Lord. From that starting point on, the book just gets progressively better. *Friend of God* should be of utmost interest to the heart of every believer. There is so much to be said about this subject, and Stony does a superb job saying it. *Friend of God* will help you fall in love with God all over again.

- **John E. Randell**

Revive Church, Edmond, OK

Introduction

I pray to my dear Lord that He gives me a long and very fulfilling life. Someday in the distant future, my life, just like yours, will come to an end if the Lord tarries. When my life is over, I want people to remember me as a man who loved his wife, his children, and his friends. But more than any of that, my greatest desire is that men will say this of me: 'He was a friend of God.'

I don't know about you, but I want to be so close to the Lord, and I want to have such a heart for God that people can look back at my life after I have left this earth and say He was indeed God's friend. That is absolutely the greatest honor that I could ever receive. It won't be that I was wealthy, famous, or powerful. It would be that I was God's friend.

Oh, friend, the best compliment for you and me would not be that we were worth a hundred billion dollars. It wouldn't be that we won all the championships that there was to win and all the gold medals that we could win. It wouldn't be that we broke every world record out there. It wouldn't even be that we had great families, that everything came easy to us, and that we had great, long, and fulfilling lives. No, the best compliment for any of us would be to be called, like Abraham, a friend of God.

That is what this book is all about. This book is born from a deep and unreserved love for my Lord and Savior. He means more to me than anything in this world. Like the song says, all that thrills my soul is Jesus and He is more than life to me.

Introduction

God is calling us to walk with Him in a deeper and more meaningful way. He wants us to get to know Him more profoundly. He doesn't desire abject and reluctant submission. He is calling us beyond subservient servanthood to a mutual bond of intimate friendship. He wants to walk with you daily just like He walked with many great men and women of old. This book is not just a manual and guide to building a friendship with God, it is a testament to who God is and how He longs for His children to pursue and seek Him with all of their hearts.

When I read through the scriptures, I find many great men and women like Noah, Abraham, Moses, Joseph, Deborah, Joshua, Esther, Daniel, David, Mary, Peter, and Paul who we have all come to know as heroes of the Bible.

What I, however, admire the most about these Biblical heroes was their love for the Lord. These men and women had such a relationship with God that the Lord Himself had compliments for some of them. Three of them stand out more prominently in relation to the topic of this book.

The first is the Patriarch, Abraham, the father of many nations. God repeatedly gives him the best compliment any man could hope to get – Friend of God. In (Isaiah 41:8), the Lord says to His people: *"But you, Israel, are My servant, Jacob whom I have chosen, The descendants of Abraham, My friend"*.

This mention of the friendship that Abraham shared with God is reinforced in the prayer of King Jehoshaphat as he faced an enemy alliance that had come up against Judah. He cried out to God saying, *"Are You not our God, who drove out the inhabitants of this land before Your people Israel, and gave it to the descendants of Abraham Your friend forever?"* (2 Chronicles 20:7).

We see this mention of Abraham being described as God's friend affirmed again in the New Testament in (James 2:23), where James declared *'And the Scripture was fulfilled which says, "Abraham believed God, and it was accounted to him for righteousness." And he was called the friend of God.'*

Abraham was so well known and described as God's friend throughout the nations of the Levant and Arabia that even the Muslims came to describe Abraham, their father (*The Arab Muslims largely proceed from the line of Ishmael, Abraham's son*) as El Khalil Allah in Arabic which translates simply as The Friend of God.

What made Abraham so dear to the Lord God of heaven that God Himself would say of Abraham – He was My friend. That is what I seek to unravel in this book.

The second figure I would like to mention is Moses. (Exodus 33:11) says, *'So the Lord spoke to Moses face to face, as a man speaks to his friend.'* You see, God was able to speak to Moses the exact same way that you speak to your spouse or friend. What caused the Lord to so befriend Moses that He would trust Moses with His manifest presence? Moses had such a friendship with the Lord that they were able to speak face-to-face. They were able to communicate continually with one another. I want to be able to speak to God like Moses spoke to God. I want to be able to hear God like Moses heard God. I want to be such a friend of God that people could say he was truly a friend of God who spoke to the Lord as a friend speaks to another friend.

Introduction

    The third Bible hero I would love to bring up is a man we can all relate to – David, the king of Israel, and Judah. While rebuking King Saul for not heeding God's commands, the prophet Samuel, speaking of David, declared, *'The Lord has sought for Himself a man after His own heart, and the Lord has commanded him to be commander over His people.'* This is reaffirmed again in (Acts 13:22), where God is quoted saying, *'I have found David the son of Jesse, a man after My own heart, who will do all My will.'* What caused God to describe a very imperfect man such as David, a man after His own heart?

These three men and many others were friends of God who always sought after the heart of God. They enjoyed such deep and intimate friendship with Yahweh Himself. They were men that we would all admire as they were all described as God's beloved. I want to be known by God and by men as a true friend of God. To me, that would be life's greatest honor. What about you? If you do also, then I welcome you to join me on this exciting journey of discovering what it means to be a friend of the Most High God.

Stony Kalango

Chapter 1

God's Friends Love Him So Dearly

*You shall love the Lord your God
with all your heart, with all your soul,
and with all your mind.* – **Matthew 22:37**

The foundation of one's friendship with the Lord is their love for the Lord. You cannot be friends with God if you don't love Him. How can you call someone a good friend when you are not fond of them? I am not talking about an acquaintance, although many Christians live their lives like God is an acquaintance. The walk that God is calling us to is one of undying love and affection. He is calling us to love Him with the entirety of our being.

He is calling to us to such a friendship in which we are constantly aware of His ever-abiding presence. He is calling us to be friends who long to be in the Secret Place with Him. He longs for friends who will desire to step into the holy of holies.

A friend of God is one whose attention is always held by the Lord. Does the underbelly of your heart cry out for communion with the living God? That is what true love for the Lord will do in you.

Wesley Wood wrote, *"To be in love with God is the high calling of the Christian. There is nothing we will do for God that can compare to the joy He takes when the ones He loves with all His being return that love to Him passionately"*.[1] As I write this, I am reminded of the

God's Friends Love Him So Dearly

song, *10,000 Reasons (Bless the Lord)* by Matt Redman. Here are some of the words to that song:

> *You're rich in love and You're slow to anger,*
> *Your Name is great and Your heart is kind;*
> *For all Your goodness I will keep on singing,*
> *Ten thousand reasons for my heart to find.*[2]

There are a million reasons that I could mention as to why I love the Lord, but one book would certainly not be enough to contain them all. What a great God we serve, that we have so many reasons to love and praise Him. I do not seek to list every reason for my love and devotion to the Lord here, as that would be impossible. I will, however, list a few in the hope that it inspires your ever-increasing faith and love for the Lord. I love the Lord because:

- He first loved me.
- He gave His life for me.
- He saved me from my sin.
- He saved me from myself.
- He saved me from my enemies.
- He spoke me into existence.
- He opens doors and opportunities that I didn't even dream about.
- He has exalted my horn like the horn of a unicorn.
- He has showered me with His all-sufficient and magnificent grace.
- He had plans for me and thought about me even before I was in my mother's womb.
- He takes good care of me.
- He watches over me.

Friend Of God

- He is always thinking about me.
- I am the Apple of His eyes.
- He cleansed me from all of my sins.
- He is my life guide and He orders the steps of my feet.
- He gave me a reason to live.
- He gave me exceeding and unspeakable joy.
- He gave me peace that the world cannot take away.
- He gave me never-ending hope.
- He gave me a blessed assurance.
- He gave me an inheritance as a saint.
- He has adopted me into His own family.
- He gave me a reason to shout for joy.
- He gave me a purpose for my life and existence.
- I am significant because of Him.
- He calls me His own.
- He bought me with His precious blood.
- He became the propitiation for all my sins.
- He replaced my guilt and shame with a warm embrace.
- He took away my mourning and replaced it with laughter and tears of joy.
- I have found Him to be the friend that sticks closer than my brothers.
- He took all my sins and tossed them to the bottom of the sea, to be remembered no more.
- He hears me when I pray and when I call upon His name.
- He made my life whole.

God's Friends Love Him So Dearly

- He gave me a new start when I didn't deserve it.
- He loved me even in spite of my sins.
- He showed me unconditional love even though He didn't need to.
- He anointed me with His power.
- He made me stand out amongst my contemporaries.
- He is my Rock; He's my firm foundation.
- I can always depend on and rely on Him.
- He is always available every second of the day when I need to call upon Him.
- He is my ever-present help in times of trouble.
- He is the answer to all of my life's questions.
- I am righteous in God's eyes because of Him.
- I've been acquitted of all my trespasses and iniquities because of Him.
- I have been justified even though I should have been found guilty.
- He has helped me face all of life's challenges that sought to shake me.
- He has kept my head above water and kept me from drowning.
- He has given me a beautiful wife and beautiful children who have become my heritage and great reward. They have become like arrows in my quiver.
- He has given my life worth, value, and significance. I am not just a random glob of cells floating randomly in space.
- He has given me knowledge and wisdom beyond my years.

Friend Of God

- He has used me as a vessel of life and hopes for others
- I have seen Him work miracle upon miracle. How can I deny Him?
- He rescued me from the plot of the devil against my life.
- He protected me from decisions that would have been devastating for me.
- He had a better plan for my life than I had for myself.
- He lifted my feet from the miry clay and set it upon a rock.
- He healed me of my diseases and sicknesses.
- He brought to reality the dreams that He put in my heart.
- He has made it possible for me to spend eternity with Him.
- He broke the shackles that kept me bound and gave me freedom and a new lease on life.
- He has turned around the lives of all those around me.
- He has done way too much good in front of my eyes.
- He saved my daughter from a miscarriage and gave her the life that she has today.
- He has taken care of and provided for my family.
- He called me His child and promised that He would always be a father to me.
- He calls me a FRIEND.

God's Friends Love Him So Dearly

A Song of Love from a King to His King

3,000 years ago, King David, the man known to be one after God's heart, wrote (Psalm 18). It is one of my favorite psalms as it captures the intensity of David's love for the Lord. I have such a deep and personal connection to this psalm, and I believe it gives you a snapshot of the reason why the Lord described David as a man after His heart. Here are the words of this splendid psalm:

1-2 "I love you, God—
 you make me strong.
God is a bedrock under my feet,
 the castle in which I live,
  my rescuing knight.

My God—the high crag
 where I run for dear life,
 hiding behind the boulders,
  safe in the granite hideout.

3 I sing to God, the Praise-Lofty,
  and find myself safe and saved.

4-5 The hangman's noose was tight at my throat;
 devil waters rushed over me.
Hell's ropes cinched me tight;
  death traps barred every exit.

6 A hostile world! I call to God,
 I cry to God to help me.
From his palace He hears my call;
 my cry brings me right into His presence—
  a private audience!

7-15 Earth wobbles and lurches;
 huge mountains shake like leaves,

Friend Of God

Quake like aspen leaves
   because of His rage.
His nostrils flare, bellowing smoke;
   His mouth spits fire.
Tongues of fire dart in and out;
   He lowers the sky.
He steps down; under His feet an abyss opens up.
He's riding a winged creature,
   swift on wind-wings.
Now He's wrapped himself
   in a trench coat of black-cloud darkness.
But His cloud-brightness bursts through,
   spraying hailstones and fireballs.
Then God thundered out of heaven;
   the High God gave a great shout,
   spraying hailstones and fireballs.
God shoots His arrows—pandemonium!
   He hurls His lightnings—a rout!
The secret sources of ocean are exposed,
   the hidden depths of earth lie uncovered
The moment you roar in protest,
      let loose your hurricane anger.

16-19 But me He caught—reached all the way
   from sky to sea; He pulled me out
Of that ocean of hate, that enemy chaos,
   the void in which I was drowning.
They hit me when I was down,
   but God stuck by me.
He stood me up on a wide-open field;
      I stood there saved—surprised to be loved!

20-24 God made my life complete
   when I placed all the pieces before him.
When I got my act together,
   He gave me a fresh start.
Now I'm alert to God's ways;

God's Friends Love Him So Dearly

    I don't take God for granted.
Every day I review the ways he works;
    I try not to miss a trick.
I feel put back together,
    and I'm watching my step.
God rewrote the text of my life
      when I opened the book of my heart to his eyes.

25-27 The good people taste your goodness,
The whole people taste your health,
The true people taste your truth,
The bad ones can't figure you out.
You take the side of the down-and-out,
    But the stuck-up you take down a notch.

28-29 Suddenly, God, you floodlight my life;
    I'm blazing with glory, God's glory!
I smash the bands of marauders,
    I vault the highest fences.

30 What a God! His road
   stretches straight and smooth.
Every God-direction is road-tested.
    Everyone who runs toward him
      Makes it.

31-42 Is there any god like God?
    Are we not at bedrock?
Is not this the God who armed me,
   then aimed me in the right direction?
Now I run like a deer;
   I'm king of the mountain.
He shows me how to fight;
   I can bend a bronze bow!
You protect me with salvation-armor;
   you hold me up with a firm hand,
   caress me with your gentle ways.

Friend Of God

You cleared the ground under me
   so, my footing was firm.
When I chased my enemies, I caught them;
   I didn't let go till they were dead men.
I nailed them; they were down for good;
   then I walked all over them.
You armed me well for this fight,
   you smashed the upstarts.
You made my enemies turn tail,
   and I wiped out the haters.
They cried "uncle"
   but Uncle didn't come;
They yelled for God
   and got no for an answer.
I ground them to dust; they gusted in the wind.
      I threw them out, like garbage in the gutter.

43-45 You rescued me from a squabbling people;
   you made me a leader of nations.
People I'd never heard of served me;
   the moment they got wind of me they listened.
The foreign devils gave up; they came
      on their bellies, crawling from their hideouts.

46-48 Live, God! Blessings from my Rock,
   my free and freeing God, towering!
This God set things right for me
   and shut up the people who talked back.
He rescued me from enemy anger,
   he pulled me from the grip of upstarts,
     He saved me from the bullies.

49-50 That's why I'm thanking you, God,
   all over the world.
That's why I'm singing songs
   that rhyme your name.
God's king takes the trophy;

God's Friends Love Him So Dearly

God's chosen is beloved.
I mean David and all His children—
    always." **(Psalm 18, MSG).**

Rooted and Grounded in the Love of God

When you become a true friend of God, you become deeply rooted and grounded in the love of God. This ability to be rooted and deeply grounded in the love of God helps you to comprehend alongside other believers what is the scope and extent of God's love. You get to understand how large the love of God is. Now, we know that the love of God has no limits; it has no boundaries. As you grow in your friendship with the Lord, you will find yourself lost in the unstoppable and unending process of discovering endless depths and the sheer enormousness of God's love. You will come to know how colossal God's love is. When believers grow in their friendship with God, they bask in the greatness of a love that knows no end.

The amazing thing about God's love is that it permeates the soul and entirety of whoever is full of it. The love of God changes us and we are never the same again. When God's love gets a hold of you, you begin to see the world in a whole new way. It brings life to your soul and body in an unexplainable manner.

You know, I can look at a preacher or worship leader and see if they are full of the love of God or if they are just being performative. One of the reasons I love worship leaders like Darlene Zschech, Alvin Slaughter, Ron Kenoly, Michael W Smith, Paul Wilbur, Kathryn Scott, Don Moen, Dunsin Onyekan, and Nathaniel Bassey is that I see the love of God permeating through when they lead worship. I mean, my list could certainly be longer, but these guys truly let their love for the Lord shine through their acts of service to the Lord. There is a marked difference between someone full of the love and presence of God and someone who is merely singing a Christian song. Anybody can sing a Christian song beautifully. Unfortunately, not everyone, however, can sing out of a place of deep connection to the Lord.

Oh, how great it is to know the love of Christ that surpasses everything. Oh, how sweet it is to be consumed by the love of God. Oh, how thrilling it is to drown daily in the love of God. I am reminded of the famous song, *Oceans* by Hillsong Worship. The lyrics read thus:

> *Spirit lead me where my trust is without borders*
> *Let me walk upon the waters*
> *Wherever You would call me*
> *Take me deeper than my feet could ever wander*
> *And my faith will be made stronger*
> *In the presence of my Savior...*[3]

When you bask in the ocean of God's love, your life is never the same again. One who drowns in God's love can never measure the depth and the height of the love of God. In that vast ocean, you get to love God so much that people will be able to say that you are a man or woman who is deeply rooted and grounded in the love of God.

In that ocean, the love of God overwhelms you. The love of God covers you up. You just swim in the love of God as a friend of God. That's how your life is supposed to be. You are just supposed to be like this tiny speckle in the midst of the oceans of God's love, and every single day, every consecutive

God's Friends Love Him So Dearly

day, it's all about knowing more and more and more and more and more about the love of God. You get to discover the love of God more and more every day. You wake up every morning and discover one new way that God loves you and how you can love Him because He loved you. That is the love of Christ. I mean, I could write a whole different book about it.

The love of Christ will gently overwhelm you if you let the Lord in. You could swim all day in that ocean of His love. This is the higher calling that Christ calls us to - oneness with the true and living God. It is unity with the Triune Godhead. It is a marriage of supernatural bliss with the Self-existent King of glory and power. That love does something in you that no man could ever do. That, my friends, is the love of God and His Christ.

I will end this chapter with these words from the eminent prince of preachers, Charles Spurgeon: "*Do you wish to be a friend of God? Well, then, first you must be fully reconciled to Him. ... Love must be created in your heart, gratitude must beget attachment, and attachment must cause delight. You must rejoice in the Lord, and maintain close communion with Him.*"[4]

Chapter 2

God's Friends Have An Indestructible Trust In The Lord.

"And those who know Your name will put their trust in You; For You, Lord, have not forsaken those who seek You." **(Psalm 9:10)**

Alexander MacLaren stated that mutual trust and confidence are *'the very lifeblood of friendship. You cannot say someone is your friend, but do not trust him. If suspicion creeps in, like the foul malaria of tropical swamps, it kills all friendship'*. Trust, faith, and confidence in God are central to true friendship with Him. God's friends have to trust God to the uttermost, and He certainly trusts those He deems to be His friends. God had such deep trust in Job that when Satan tried to convince God that Job only feared God because He blessed and protected him; God allowed Satan to test that trust. God knew what the outcome would be from the start because Job was such a friend of God. Can God trust you enough to let Satan afflict you, knowing that you would still maintain your deep and undying trust and confidence in Him?

In this chapter, I want to put the spotlight on a few Bible heroes who are excellent examples of God's friends who displayed unshakable trust in the Lord. The story of these individuals will inspire your love and trust in the Lord as they have done for millions of saints all throughout history.

God's Friends Have An Indestructible Trust In The Lord.

Abraham

When you think of a man who God called His friend, it is hard to think past the great Patriarch and father of many nations, Abraham. God Himself called Abraham His friend, and many generations throughout human history have referred to the servant of God from the land of Ur, which is today about 2000 miles southeast of modern-day Baghdad in Iraq, as the same. Abraham was such a friend of God that God plagued the house of Pharaoh for taking in Sarah, who Abraham had freely offered up to them in order to spare his life.

While Abraham was still in his father's house, God called him to leave, saying:

> *"Get out of your country, From your family*
> *And from your father's house,*
> *To a land that I will show you.*
> *I will make you a great nation;*
> *I will bless you and make your name great;*
> *And you shall be a blessing.*
> *I will bless those who bless you,*
> *And I will curse him who curses you;*
> *And in you all the families of the earth shall be blessed."* **(Genesis 12:1-3)**

Abraham obeyed and trusted God even though he didn't know where God was taking Him. Can you imagine leaving the security and safety of all you know and love to embark on a quest without a stated end goal? In this act, Abraham showed deep trust in the Lord and believed that what God had promised him would come to pass. Friends, simple trust, and obedience to the Lord do many wonders.

Friend Of God

Abraham again displayed faith and trust in the Lord when he let Lot, his nephew, take the seemingly better grazing land when it was time for him and Lot, alongside their servants, to split up. Abraham trusted more in the promise God had given than the obvious fertile physical land of milk and honey that he could have rightfully claimed as his own. To Abraham, God was his source and supply.

Abraham trusted the Lord when he decided to pay a tithe to Melchizedek, King of Salem and priest of the Most High God. I strongly believe that the priest Melchizedek spoken of in scripture refers to the Pre-Incarnate Christ.

Abraham trusted the Lord again after he had emerged victorious in his battle against a coalition of kings that had come up against Sodom, Gomorrah, Admah, Zeboiim, and Bela. Now, this was before the land of Sodom and Gomorrah was destroyed by the Lord for their vile immorality and wickedness. Abraham got into the war because his nephew Lot had been captured by the coalition army of Chedorlaomer, king of Elam; Tidal, king of nations; Amraphel, king of Shinar; and Arioch, king of Ellasar. After the victory, the king of Sodom tried to reward Abraham for his help in being victorious over the enemy. Abraham, a man who saw God as his only source, said to the king of Sodom: "*I have raised my hand to the Lord, God Most High, the Possessor of heaven and earth, that I will take nothing, from a thread to a sandal strap, and that I will not take anything that is yours, lest you should say, 'I have made Abram rich'*" (Genesis 14:22-23). For Abraham, the earthly rewards of riches and prestige given by an earthly king weren't comparable to the blessings of His God. He wanted no one but the Lord to get the glory.

God's Friends Have An Indestructible Trust In The Lord.

Abraham trusted and obeyed God again when the Lord instructed him to circumcise every male member of his household as a sign of the covenant between Abraham and the Lord. Can you imagine going through the process of circumcision when you are ninety-nine years old? The amazing thing about this circumcision story is that he obeyed God in circumcising every male member of his household on the very same day that God gave him that instruction. He didn't wait an extra day or an extra week. He obeyed God instantly and was quick to perform what the Lord had instructed him to do. That, my friends, is what you call a display of total trust in obedience to God almighty.

Abraham again trusted God when God promised him that he and Sarah would give birth to a child at a very old age. At this time, Abraham was 99 years old, and his wife, Sarah, was 90 years old. Scientists say that the average age for a woman's menopause is 51 years old. Despite this, God told Abraham that Sarah, who was almost forty years past her childbearing years, would have a son. It takes a lot of faith and trust to believe in something that is not biologically possible. Abraham, being a friend of God, however, knew the God he served.

Now, his wife, Sarah, had a different reaction to God's promise of a child being born to them through her. The scriptures say she *"laughed within herself, saying, "After I have grown old, shall I have pleasure, my lord being old also?"* (Genesis 18:12). In that interaction, you see the difference between a regular child of God and one who is a friend of God. The friend of God believes a thing because God said it, even if they struggle to understand it. A child of God who is not a true friend of

God will respond just as a rational skeptic would. A friend of God, however, knows that nothing is too hard for God.

Abraham trusted God again after Isaac had been born and grown in age. Of all the situations in which Abraham had to trust fully in God, this was the hardest. Isaac, who was Abraham's miracle child from God, was certainly a child loved dearly by his father, given that he was his heir and was the fulfillment of his long-awaited and promised reward from God. Isaac was very valuable to his father and mother who had brought forth this child in their very old age. God asked Abraham for the hardest sacrifice of all. The scriptures say God appeared again to Abraham and said: *"Take now your son, your only son Isaac, whom you love, and go to the land of Moriah, and offer him there as a burnt offering on one of the mountains of which I shall tell you.*"

Now, I don't know about you, but I know that this would be the hardest instruction to ever obey. Now, you might think that even though Abraham eventually carried out this instruction, he probably grudgingly did it. If you thought that, you would be wrong. Abraham was such a friend of God that obeying and trusting in God was more important than the life of his highly cherished son. I am pretty sure that Abraham didn't mention what he was about to do to his wife. He just charged head-on with God's command to him. The scriptures say, "*Abraham rose early in the morning and saddled his donkey, and took two of his young men with him, and Isaac his son; and he split the wood for the burnt offering, and arose and went to the place of which God had told him.*"

When Isaac asked Abraham, his father, where the lamb that would be used for the sacrifice was, Abraham told him

God's Friends Have An Indestructible Trust In The Lord.

that God would provide for Himself. That line is where we get the name of God, *Jehovah Jireh,* from. Just as he was about to slay his son on that mountain, offering him up as a sacrifice to God, a voice came from heaven saying, *"Do not lay your hand on the lad, or do anything to him; for now, I know that you fear God, since you have not withheld your son, your only son, from Me."* God provided a lamb in the thickest of the bush nearby as the sacrifice for Abraham in place of his son. God Himself saw the trust that Abraham had in Him and was pleased with Abraham's ever-yielding obedience. Wow, what an act of selfless faith and trust in the Lord that Abraham showed. Can you trust and obey God as Abraham did? That is what it takes for God to call you His friend.

As you look throughout Abraham's life, you can see such a display of faith and trust in God over and over again. It wasn't an act of faith and belief here and there. No, Abraham's entire life was a formidable display of His faith and trust in His everlasting God. This continual and unending faith and trust in God that Abraham displayed was at the center of his life. He knew nothing else but unquestionable trust in his Lord and King. MacLaren described that trust in this manner:

> *But whilst we know that this belief in God was the very nerve and centre of Abraham's whole character, and was the reason why he was called the friend of God, we must also remember that, as James insists upon here, it was no mere idle assent, no mere intellectual conviction that God could not tell lies, which was dignified by the name of belief, but that it was, as James insists upon in the context, a trust which proved itself to be valid, because it was continually operative in the life.*

David

A friend of God has true faith in God. Our faith and trust in God is built on our love for Him. Let it be known *'that the heavenly and the earthly friend, like friends on the low levels of humanity, love each other because they trust each other.'* David displayed such formidable faith and trust in the Lord when he decided to take on the giant, Goliath with only a sling and five stones. To David, the size of Goliath meant nothing. He knew and trusted his Lord, the God of Israel. That was all that David knew he needed in order to emerge victorious. King Saul and most of the army of Israel cowered in fear for many days as Goliath and the Philistines taunted them and blasphemed the God of Israel. If they had been God's friends, they would have shown the same trust in God that David did; rather, they looked at their abilities alone and did not look to the Lord. They were leaning on their capabilities and understanding and not on the Lord. In his matchup against Goliath, David, appearing without any armor, spoke these words to his gigantic enemy:

"You come to me with a sword, with a spear, and with a javelin. But I come to you in the name of the LORD of hosts, the God of the armies of Israel, whom you have defied. This day the LORD will deliver you into my hand, and I will strike you and take your head from you. And this day I will give the carcasses of the camp of the Philistines to the birds of the air and the wild beasts of the earth, that all the earth may know that there is a God in Israel". **(1 Samuel 17:45-46).**

It's only one who is a friend of God and has such trust in His maker that would make such a statement as David did. God rewarded the trust that David had in Him and gave David a thumping and resounding victory over his enemies. This same David who spent his life trusting in the Lord, at a future

God's Friends Have An Indestructible Trust In The Lord.

date proclaimed: *"Some trust in and boast of chariots and some of horses, but we will trust in and boast of the name of the Lord our God."* (Psalm 20:7 Amplified Classic Version). David was a friend of God, and a hallmark of that friendship was his undying and ironclad trust in God.

Job

The story of Job is known by most Christians. He was a righteous man who deeply feared the Lord. Despite this, the Lord allowed calamity to fall upon him to prove to the devil that Job, his humble servant, would never turn his back on the Lord. Job was a wealthy man who seemed to have everything a man desired, but his life took a very wild turn towards total disaster. He lost everything he had, from his wealth to his health, prestige, and even his family. Despite all of the terrible ill fortune, Job never lost trust and faith in God. Amid all his afflictions, he declared: *"Though He slay me, yet will I trust Him"* (Job 13:15).

Job's wife was not like Job. Satan struck Job with the most painful boils possible. His health was a disaster, and he was indeed in an utterly miserable state. Looking at his cataclysmic plight, his wife said to him: *"Do you still hold fast to your integrity? Curse God and die!"* Job, who knew and trusted his Maker more than the situation he was in, responded to her saying, *"You speak as one of the foolish women speaks. Shall we indeed accept good from God, and shall we not accept adversity?"*

Through all his adversities, the Scriptures said this of Job: *"In all this Job did not sin with his lips."* His wife wanted a friend of God to walk away from God because of the terrible misfortune that he was experiencing, but Job knew better. He knew that the mutual bond of friendship that He had with

God could not be broken. He trusted God way too much to let physical disaster be the bringer of ruin to that trust. He knew that God, who had allowed all of the misfortune to happen, was the same God who could turn everything around in one second. Such was Job's trust in the Lord. His trust in the Lord was greater than anything else. This trust is what he expressed when he said:

> *I know that my redeemer lives,*
> *and that in the end he will stand on the earth.*
> *And after my skin has been destroyed,*
> *yet in my flesh I will see God;*
> *I myself will see him*
> *with my own eyes—I, and not another.*
> *How my heart yearns within me!*
> **(Job 19:25-27)**

Noah

I want you to put yourself in Noah's shoes for a brief moment. At a time when there had never been a major flood in the history of the world, God told him that there would be a historic flood that would happen that would end the existence of most life around the earth for a few weeks. I can imagine the mockery that Noah and his family would have faced as they built this ark. Everyone around Noah would have thought he was crazy, stupid, and probably a lunatic. Everyone would have tried to preach to him about the eventual futility of his actions. If anyone else apart from his family had believed, they would have joined him in the ark, but no one did. They would have thought for years that Noah was an idiotic loser. All of the possible opposition did not stop Noah from completing what God had instructed him to do.

God's Friends Have An Indestructible Trust In The Lord.

Could God have just spoken a wooden ark into existence and spared Noah the sweat, toil, abundant patience, and resolve? Yes, God was capable of doing so, but God wants His friends to display their trust in Him by obedience to His words even when they sound foolish. Noah trusted God through all of it, and in return, God restarted the course of human history through this friend of His who trusted wholly in His promises. God's friends trust the Lord with all of their hearts. I will close this chapter with this beautiful scripture:

"Trust in the Lord with all your heart,
And lean not on your own understanding;
In all your ways acknowledge Him,
And He shall direct your paths.
Do not be wise in your own eyes;
Fear the Lord and depart from evil."
(Proverbs 3:5-7)

Chapter 3

God's Friends Walk In The Fear Of The Lord

"There was a man in the land of Uz whose name was Job; and that man was blameless and upright, and one who feared God [with reverence] and abstained from and turned away from evil [because he honored God]" **(Job 1:1 AMP).**

God's friends have a profound and reverential fear of the Lord. One of the greatest things the modern church has largely lost is our knowledge and expression of the fear of the Lord. And it's because we've lost the fear of God that we, at times, seem to be heading in the wrong direction.

So, what then is the fear of the Lord? The Hebrew word for the fear of the Lord is *Yirah Adonai. Adonai* refers to *God the Lord* in Hebrew, and the word *Yirah* is only used in relation to a particular fear – the fear of the Divine, which is the fear of the Lord. The fear of the Lord is simply defined as the holy wonder, awe, and reverence of God.

19th-century preacher and theologian, Charles Bridges defined the fear of the Lord as '*that affectionate reverence, by which the child of God bends himself humbly and carefully to his Father's law.*'[1] The fear of the Lord speaks of holy reverence for God. It deals with your posture when it comes to honoring your Creator. When I speak of the fear of the Lord, I don't mean fear as in terror or being petrified. It's not fear in the sense of you being

God's Friends Walk In The Fear Of The Lord

afraid like God is going to kill or destroy you. No. The fear of the Lord speaks about holy awe. It denotes you standing in awe and wonder at how holy, great, glorious, and majestic your God is. In your awe of His indescribable nature, you express deep and heartfelt reverence for God.

God's intention is for us to draw closer to Him. A man who knows and loves God fears God. Such a person is not scared of God but is in awe of God. With the fear of the Lord, your response to God is not: '*God, I'm afraid of you. You're going to kill me. You're going to judge and punish me.*' Instead, it is: *My God, you are amazing. My God, you are powerful. My God, you are great and greatly to be praised. Great are your works in all the earth. My soul sings hallelujah.*'

This fear is completely different from the fear of man. Jesus said, 'Do *not fear those who kill the body but cannot kill the soul. But rather fear Him who is able to destroy both soul and body in hell.*' (Matthew 10:28).

We ought not to fear man, but we ought to fear God just like the apostles. The great English philosopher and statesman, Edmund Burke said '*He that fears God fears nothing else*'[2]. The man who fears God has nothing to fear. The man who fears God will not fear man. The fear of the Lord displaces the fear of man. King David rightly said "*In God, whose word I praise, in God I trust; I will not be afraid. What can mere mortals do to me?*" (Psalm 56:4 CSB).

On one of my drives to work one morning, I was listening to an audio narration of the Book of Acts. In chapter 5, there is a powerful story of the apostles being arrested a second time after they were unjustly found guilty of preaching the gospel.

Friend Of God

In a gathering of the Sanhedrin, they were again reprimanded for their bold proclamation of Christ. The high priest of the council said to the apostles: *"We gave you strict orders never again to teach in this man's name! Instead, you have filled all Jerusalem with your teaching about him, and you want to make us responsible for his death!"* In response to the high priest, Peter, and the apostles said, *"We must obey God rather than men."* Gamaliel appealed, warning the Sanhedrin that if the apostles were of God, nothing they would do would suppress God's work. After this appeal by Gamaliel, the council let the apostles go with another warning not to preach in the name of Jesus Christ. Did they obey the orders of the Sanhedrin? Of course, they didn't. Rather, they *'left the high council rejoicing that God had counted them worthy to suffer disgrace for the name of Jesus. And every day, in the Temple and from house to house, they continued to teach and preach this message: "Jesus is the Messiah."*

This story rightly presents the striking contrasts between the fear of man and the fear of the Lord. They had no fear of men even as they were threatened with their own lives. They feared and revered God too much to allow the threats of men to stop them from proclaiming the Good news of Jesus the Messiah. They didn't care about the hostile threats and condemnation of men. They feared God so much that they were filled with joy because they were counted worthy to suffer for their faith in the Lord Jesus. John Witherspoon was right when he said *'It is only the fear of God that can deliver us from the fear of man'*.[3]

The fear of man and the fear of God are two different things. The fear of God is not casual fear. And in fact, we know it to be true from Scripture, that God does not like fear. (1 John 4:18) says, *'There is no fear in love; but perfect love casts out fear, because fear involves torment. But he who fears has not been made perfect in love.'*

Funny enough, the fear of the Lord is actually the complete and total opposite of the fear of anything else. The reason is that God wants you to fear Him alone and nobody else. Fear is an emotion that's supposed to be positively directed to only one entity: God, not things, not death, not sickness, not people, not the devil, not demons, not evil. God is the only worthy recipient of your fear. And when God is the recipient of your fear, the motivation for your fear is not that you are petrified. It's not that you are scared. It is that you love and adore Him.

Think about a phobia that you or someone else might have. Some people have a fear of heights. Others dread public speaking, or swimming, or certain animals. The fear of things emerges from your knowledge of or an encounter with the thing that you fear. That knowledge or encounter instills in you a certain emotion that makes you balk at that thing or run away from it. We tend to shy away from whatever it is that we are afraid of. That is the human stimuli response. So, if you're afraid of heights, you're going to stay away from high-rise buildings. If you are afraid of water, you're not going to want to jump into a lake. If you are afraid of skydiving, you're not going to want to get into a plane, go up 10,000 feet in the air, and try to jump out of that plane. Your fear keeps you away from the object of your fear. Your fear creates a distance between you and the thing that you are afraid of.

However, when the Bible speaks about the fear of the Lord, it's a completely different concept. This type of fear is fear that brings you closer to God. It's your fear of the Lord that enables you to gain proximity to Him. The fear of the Lord doesn't cause you to ignore or try to create a distance between yourself and God. For everything else, the fear of those things pushes you away and not closer. The biblical fear of God, however, draws you nearer to God.

Your fear of God is born out of your love of God.

Fearing God means you admire Him so much that you want to do everything to please Him. Fearing God means you honor God in all that you do. That means first that you honor God physically with your body. The Bible says, 'Dear *brothers and sisters, I plead with you to give your bodies to God because of all he has done for you. Let them be a living and holy sacrifice—the kind he will find acceptable. This is truly the way to worship him.*' (Romans 12:1 NLT).

That's why you don't do anything with your body that you know dishonors God. Fearing the Lord also means that you honor God with your resources, whether that's your finances, tithes, offerings, or giving to the poor, the wrongfully persecuted, and the unfortunate. Your resources could also be your time or your efforts rendered to the work of the Lord.

Fearing the Lord means you honor God with your soul and spirit. It means that you honor God with everything that you have within you. Fearing God means respecting God and seeing Him as the Lord of your life. It means seeing Him as the author and finisher of your faith, as the one that you can do nothing without, and as the Alpha and Omega in your life.

The Fear of the Lord brings the Presence of the Lord

God's manifest presence only shows up in a place where He is revered or worshiped. His manifest presence always shows up only when He is enthroned in the praises of His people. God will not show up in His manifest presence in the midst of carnal chaos and selfishness. That's why when you worship, you focus on Him and nothing else. You shut everything out because He is worthy of your time and full attention. And sometimes, we Christians have forgotten that.

We have forgotten that the fear of the Lord is utter reverence for the Lord. It's to stand in awe of the great and mighty Emperor of the Universe. (Joshua 4:24 AMP) says, *'That all the peoples of the earth may know that the hand of the Lord is mighty and that you may reverence and fear the Lord your God forever.'*

Your reverence for God is a response to your revelation of God. You only gain reverence for one who you truly know or who you've truly seen. When God reveals Himself, or as I like to say it – When God shows up, the only response should be reverence for Him. That's how it always was in the Bible, and that should always be our response when God's presence shows up.

I can imagine you have read or heard of the story of Moses in the burning bush. In the moment that God appeared to Moses, He told him, *'Take off your shoes, for this is holy ground.* Not every ground is holy ground. A ground becomes holy because the manifest presence of God is revealed.

Holy Awe and Wonder

I want you to take a moment and imagine yourself as Yuri Gagarin in April 1961, becoming the first man to ever go into space. Just imagine what he would have felt as he orbited the Earth from outer space. As the first man ever to do that, he saw, felt, and experienced what no one in all of human history had ever experienced. Imagine his reaction as he looked at the billions of miles of empty, dark space without gravity that no man had ever seen before. What would have come into his mind? Imagine the awe he had in that moment of God's limitless universe.

Imagine yourself for a moment as Neil Armstrong and Buzz Aldrin, the first men to ever set foot on the moon. We all know the famous first words spoken on the moon: That's *one small step for man, one giant leap for mankind.* Now, think about the awe they experienced in that moment.

Imagine yourself as Edmund Hillary and the Sherpa guide, Tenzing Norgay, the first men to successfully climb to the top of Mount Everest, which is the tallest mountain on earth, at 29,031.69 feet (8,848.86 meters). Think about the awe they felt and experienced in that moment when they would have said to themselves: *We have gotten to the top of the world.* They had gotten to a point on earth that no man had ever approached. What a breathtaking moment that was as they made history looking at a world where they stood higher than anything on planet Earth.

Friends, now think of the awe and wonder of the God of heaven and earth, the Creator of everything that exists. When I think about the majestic and glorious nature of my Lord and Savior, a favorite worship song of mine comes to mind, and it is called *I Stand in Awe of You.* Here are the words to that song:

> *You are beautiful beyond description*
> *Too marvelous for words*
> *Too wonderful for comprehension*
> *Like nothing ever seen or heard*
> *Who can grasp Your infinite wisdom?*

God's Friends Walk In The Fear Of The Lord

Who can fathom the depth of Your love?
You are beautiful beyond description
Majesty, enthroned above
And I stand, I stand in awe of You
I stand, I stand in awe of You
Holy God, to whom all praise is due
I stand in awe of You[4]

That song speaks of the awe and fear of the Lord. When we stand before our God, we can't help but be in breathtaking awe of Him in His majesty, beauty, and glory. The human English vocabulary does not have enough words to describe how great and powerful our God is. When you get into a place of worship and stillness in His presence and you long to see His face, you are not bothered about anything else but the Lord. Friends, this is what it means to have the fear of the Lord.

The forgotten yet essential Ingredient

The church talks about the love of God so much, and that's a good thing. The love of God is a foundational pillar of who God is. But we easily forget to talk about the fear of the Lord. Sadly, it breaks my heart anytime I read or hear the news of sexual and financial scandals in the body of Christ. You've got many people who claim to serve the Lord, yet they don't steward God's money in a way that pleases Him and brings glory to His name. Some preachers and church staff members embezzle church funds without a care in the world. They use up God's money like it's their own and do not fear God enough to walk in righteousness, accountability, and integrity.

They may love God, but they certainly don't fear Him. If you feared God, you wouldn't spend God's money on frivolous stuff. The other day, I was watching a video of secular dancers paid to dance provocatively in God's house. I mean, this was a mega church in Chicago that spent God's money in such a way that truly dishonors the Lord. They certainly did not have the fear of the Lord. God's friends would know better because they possess the fear of the Lord.

God's friends have a healthy fear of the Lord. Every hour of the day, in heaven, angels bow before God's throne saying, *holy, holy, holy is the Lord God Almighty*. Doesn't that just cause you to be in a state of awe? Everybody in scripture who had a glimpse of the presence of God had a reaction in which they were astonished. God's presence will mesmerize you beyond reasoning.

When Isaiah and Ezekiel saw visions of the Lord, they were blown away. They were completely overwhelmed. I am talking about the Omnipresent, Omniscient, and Omnipotent God. I am talking about the only great, mighty, and wise God. His throne is the governmental center of the whole universe. The Bible says His eyes burn with fire. His feet are like burning brass. His hair is white as wool. The roads of His heaven are paved with gold as asphalt. A God who has millions of angels worshiping Him daily, obeying His every bidding and hanging on to His every word. Just one of those angels in the Bible was sent by God, and he slew 185,000 Assyrian enemy soldiers that had come up against Israel in one night. Friends, that is the God we serve, and He should be the only subject of our fear.

God highly treasures our Fear of Him

Speaking of the Messiah who was to be revealed on the Earth at a future time, which is Jesus Christ, the Prophet Isaiah declared: '*He will delight in the fear of the Lord*' (Isaiah 11:3). Now, pause for a second and dwell on that. The delight of our Lord and Savior will be the fear of the Lord. So, the fear of the Lord matters to Jesus very much, not a little, not somewhat. It matters to Him a lot. Doesn't that tell you how much the fear of the Lord means to the heart of God? Jerry Bridges said *'If Jesus in his humanity delighted in the fear of God, surely, we need to give serious thought to cultivating this attitude in our lives'*.[5]

Do you know what it means to delight in something? It means to relish in something, and enjoy doing it. It means to love doing something so much. If you love Jesus and seek to be a friend of His, you ought to highly value the fear of the Lord. You ought to value the fear of the Lord just like David did. David's fear and reverence for the Lord was one of the key reasons why we know him as the man who was after God's very heart.

David refused to kill King Saul, despite having multiple chances to do so, simply because he feared God too much. He did not chase his personal ambitions, even though it was his right to kill the man who had tirelessly sought to kill him. For David, what mattered most was the fact that God had ordained Saul to be the king of Israel, and he wasn't going to destroy that because doing so would be destroying God's anointed, and David wanted none of that.

This was despite the fact that David was himself now anointed by the Prophet Samuel to be the true king of Israel. Even then, David valued the fact that Saul, at one point, was anointed by God as king. It wasn't Saul himself that David respected. It was the calling of God on Saul that David respected and honored, and even the opportunity to eliminate his biggest threat wasn't more important than His regard for

Friend Of God

what God had anointed. Oh, how I pray that God's children, who now live under a much better covenant, would honor and reverentially fear God just like David did. In doing so, the Lord will also testify of us that we were friends of His, who were after His very own heart.

Isaiah also declared that the fear of the Lord is God's own treasure (Isaiah 33:6 Complete Jewish Bible). It's not something he just casually likes or deems sort of important. It's what God delights in. It's what Jesus delights in. This posture truly matters to God. And because it matters to God, it should matter to you and to me. It should certainly mean a lot to you if you ever want to be called a friend of God.

God delights in those who fear Him

In (Psalms 25:12-13), we are asked a question: *"Who is the man that fears the Lord? Him shall He teach in the way He chooses. He himself shall dwell in prosperity, and his descendants shall inherit the earth."*

Are you a man or woman who fears God? You are the one that God says will be taught by Himself. Only those who fear the Lord will be taught by God. God will not teach somebody who does not fear Him. He's just not going to do that. Only those who possess a reverential fear of the Lord can call themselves friends of God. God doesn't delight in a man who lacks respect for Him. The Scriptures say, *'God opposes the proud but shows favor to the humble.'* (James 4:6 NIV).

The Psalmist in that same 25th chapter of Psalms goes on to declare that *'The secret of the Lord is with those who fear Him, And He will show them His covenant.'* (Psalm 25:14). Do you want to get a hold of the secrets of God? Do you want the Holy

God's Friends Walk In The Fear Of The Lord

Spirit to reveal to you the mysteries of God, the deeper things of God, the hidden secrets of God? Do you want to learn more about God than you've ever known? Do you want to know God in a deeper and more meaningful way? Do you want to encounter the mighty presence of our great God? I tell you then: You must have the fear of the Lord. That's the key. You must have a deep, reverential fear of God. You must have a deep honor for Him and who He is. You must have a deep reverence for Him as the creator of the world, as King of kings and Lord of lords, as master of the universe, and as the soon and coming king.

If you fear the Lord, He will share His secrets with you. In the story of Abraham and Lot, we see an example of two seemingly righteous men; however, only one truly feared God. Both Abraham and Lot were righteous, but Lot was not a friend of God. Abraham, however, truly was a friend of God. Lot was righteous. In fact, when Abraham prayed and said: *If there's any righteous man in Sodom, will you spare them*, was mainly referring to Lot and his family. They were going to be the only righteous people saved from the destruction of Sodom and Gomorrah. But Lot did not fear God. He didn't honor God.

There are lots of Christians like Lot. I meet them all the time. Through their actions, they say: *I love Jesus, but I want to do my own thing. I love Jesus, but I want to live my life how I want to. I love Jesus, but I will vote for and support the devil's agenda on this earth.*

Think about this. You only share secrets with people who you trust, right? You don't just share secrets with every acquaintance of yours. You share your secrets with somebody that you trust. It's the same way with God. He's going to only share secrets of the future and of the present with those friends of His who fear Him. He's only going to speak deeper things to people who fear Him. So, if you don't fear God, you are likely not going to hear the voice of the Lord. But if you fear God, He will speak to you. He will make Himself known to you. He'll reveal Himself to you.

The Fear of the Lord helps you delight in God's Commands

The fear of God promotes spiritual joy; it is the morning star that ushers in the sunlight of comfort.[6]
– Thomas Watson

Jesus said, *He who loves me keeps my commands* (John 14:21). Having the fear of the Lord will help you delight in the laws of God. Now, there's a difference between just obeying God and delighting in obeying God. Some Christians do certain things only because that's all they've ever known. Some Christians do certain things only because the pastor says they should do it. Some Christians do certain things because other Christians are doing and they just feel like they ought to also do it. You should not obey God just because it's a nice thing to do. You should obey God because you delight in His commands. See, that's the difference between a burdensome Christian life and a Christian life that's full of joy. If you are Christian and your Christian walk is not full of joy and peace, it's because you are not delighting in the Lord. Your delight is not in the commandments of God, so it's a burden for you. That, however, is not how our Christian life should be. Our Christian life should be such that we always walk around with a smile on our face. Why? It's because we know Jesus saved

God's Friends Walk In The Fear Of The Lord

and redeemed us. When God puts His spirit in you, it is to help you delight and obey His commands.

> *To how many of us is the very notion of religion that of a prohibition of things that we would much like to do, and of commands to do things that we had much rather not do? All the slavery of abject submission, of reluctant service, is clean swept away, when we understand that friendship and love find their supreme delight in discovering and in executing the will of the beloved. And surely if you and I are the friends of God, the cold words, 'duty,' 'must,' 'should,' will be struck out of our vocabulary and will be replaced by 'delight,' 'cannot but; 'will.' For friends find the very life - I was going to say the voice-of their friendship in mutual obedience.[7]*
> **– Alexander Maclaren**

The Lord promised Moses that sometime in the future, He would not write His laws on tablets of stone; rather, He would write them in our hearts. That prophecy has been fulfilled today. God is not just all about the Bible as a book. The book itself, which is left unopened, is completely useless. True life is found in the opened book whose words have leaped from the pages of the book into your spirit. The word of God on the printed page does nothing. The word of God in you is what does everything.

The Fear of the Lord will keep you away from sin and iniquity

> *As the embankment keeps out the water, so, the fear of the Lord keeps out uncleanness.[8]*
> **- Thomas Watson**

> *"In mercy and truth, Atonement is provided for iniquity;*

Friend Of God

And by the fear of the Lord one departs from evil."
(Proverbs 16:6)

Everybody struggles with sin but the individual who has the fear of the Lord tries to stay away from sin because they know that it doesn't please God. Sin doesn't bring any glory to God. The fear of the Lord keeps you away from iniquity. When the fear of the Lord is present in your life and in your heart, sin, and iniquity will be far away from you. If you fear God, He will lift you up and give you the strength to overcome sin. He will keep you in perfect peace. If you fear God, you will come to know Him in a more profound way. You just have to fear Him, know Him, and see Him for who He is. Don't cheapen your view of God. God is still holy and righteous and tells us to depart from iniquity.

The fear of the Lord matters so much to God, and it matters so much to Jesus that the Lord's Prayer literally starts by saying, *Our Father who art in heaven, hallowed be your name*. When you pray, as Jesus instructed us to pray, you automatically begin by recognizing God for who He is. You see and acknowledge how awesome and majestic He is. He is not just your Father. He is your heavenly Father.

At the start of this chapter, we read about Job, a man who feared God and shunned evil. What does it mean to shun evil? It means to run away from evil. It means to not even consider evil because you want to please and honor God. You do so because you want the Lord to look at you and say, '*Look at my daughter, look at my son, in whom I'm well pleased*'. It's the fear of God that causes you not to sin. Do you fear God, or do you

God's Friends Walk In The Fear Of The Lord

have opinions in your life that you know contradict the word of God, and yet you still hold on to them?

Those who abandon their faith and walk away from the Lord do so because they've lost or never had the fear of the Lord. Some Christians don't care whatsoever about the institution of marriage and what it means and symbolizes. They choose to just do whatever they feel like doing. That, my friend, is due to the lack of fear of the Lord. Do you know what causes immorality and sin to thrive? It is the lack of the fear of the Lord.

We've lost the fear of God in our societies, not just in America but all around the world. And because we've lost the fear of the Lord, sin, and immorality thrives. You see, whenever the Israelites lost the fear of the Lord, they fell into sin. That was always what happened. They would lose the fear of the Lord, and then they would fall into sin. When they repented and regained the fear of the Lord, sin was gone, and God would save them.

Do you admire your Lord? I see some of the things that fellow Christians do, and it baffles me. I ask myself, where is the fear of God? I am not trying to come off as holier than thou. I am challenging you to live your life with the fear of the Lord. Oh, how we need the fear of God in our lives again. I am so convicted about this.

We've lost the fear of God in our churches, in our ministries, and in how we handle church finances and relationships. I hear all the time about church splits that happen because somebody wants to implement their own agenda, and they would rather let the church sink and fail than not have their way. And they never pull back and think: *how about us wanting God's way?* It may not be the worship style you like, but do you fear God enough not to derail the cause of Christ? Some people don't care because they don't have the fear of the Lord. I ask myself, how you have churches where church members threaten a pastor, saying: *If you don't do things my way, I'll leave with my money.* How dare you? Do you not care that you could be in opposition to God's interests? I never want to be in God's way; instead, I want to always move in congruence with Him, so your prayer should be: *Lord if I am in opposition to your will, correct me.*

Oh, how I pray that we, as God's children, as the body of Christ, will regain a healthy fear of the Lord. When we have a healthy fear of the Lord, we are saying we honor and respect Him. We are saying that He deserves all the glory and the honor and praise. We are saying that no gift we give Him will be enough to describe how wondrous He is. The fear of the Lord, my friends, is key to becoming a true friend of God. God's friends embody a deep and reverential fear of God. John Bevere rightly said *'Holy fear is the key to God's sure foundation, unlocking the treasuries of salvation, wisdom, and knowledge. Along with the love of God, it composes the very foundation of life!'*[9]

I will end this chapter with this verse from Moses as he spoke to the people of Israel about what the Lord required of them and, by extension, us.

"And now, Israel, what does the Lord your God require of you, but to fear the Lord your God, to walk in all His ways and to love Him, to serve the Lord your God with all your heart and with all your soul." (Deuteronomy 10:12).

Chapter 4

God Is Pleased With His Friends

"Then the Lord saw that the wickedness of man was great in the earth, and that every intent of the thoughts of his heart was only evil continually. And the Lord was sorry that He had made man on the earth, and He was grieved in His heart. So the Lord said, "I will destroy man whom I have created from the face of the earth, both man and beast, creeping thing and birds of the air, for I am sorry that I have made them." But Noah found grace in the eyes of the Lord. This is the genealogy of Noah. Noah was a just man, perfect in his generations. Noah walked with God."
(Genesis 6:5-8).

God is pleased with His friends. He's also delighted with His friends. In the scripture above, there is a great observation to be made. We see the almighty Creator of heaven and earth in a moment of deliberation.

There are only a few moments in scripture where God deliberates on what He's done, and this is one of them. God was looking into the earth, and He saw great sin. He saw that everybody had gone their own way. He saw that everybody was doing their own thing. He saw that everyone lived wickedly and performed vile sins. He saw that everyone was basically doing what they wanted to do, and they were not thinking about what pleased or delighted God and what didn't.

Friend Of God

It sounds a lot like our modern world. They were just doing what they wanted to do, and the Bible says God was sorry. He was sorry that He had made man; He was sad.

He was displeased and disheartened, but in the midst of all this, the Bible says that Noah found grace in the eyes of the Lord. This means that God was pleased with Noah, and this was because Noah was a friend of His. In the same moment that we learn that God was sad with what He saw in the world, we also learn that He was delighted with one man. What made this man different from the others? What caused this man to be a source of delight and gladness to the Lord when He was full of sorrow and regret as He looked across the earth?

The difference between this man and the multitude who were engaged in iniquity was that Noah was a friend of God who had a heart after the Lord and the others were enemies of God who only sought to do what was right in their own eyes. They didn't think or consider what God wanted from them. They only thought of what was right and pleasing in their own eyes.

Noah, however, was different. He was a friend of God who cared about what God cared about, and so, even in a moment when the God of the universe felt sad about the human race, a friend of His who was also a man brought joy to His heart. Friend, I long to be a man who brings joy to the heart of the Lord when He looks upon the earth. You know, the Lord may look on America and the world today and see so much filth and iniquity, but in the midst of all of that, can you be the standout individual like Noah who brings a smile to His face?

God Is Pleased With His Friends

Let's read a scripture where we see Jesus pleasing God the Father. The context is the baptism of Jesus by John the Baptist in the River Jordan: *"When He had been baptized, Jesus came up immediately from the water; and behold, the heavens were opened to Him, and He saw the Spirit of God descending like a dove and alighting upon Him. And suddenly a voice came from heaven, saying, "This is My beloved Son, in whom I am well pleased."* (Matthew 3:16-17).

What a profound commendation those words were from God the Father. What a remark of pride from God on His Son, Jesus Christ. May those words: (*This is My beloved Son, in whom I am well pleased*) resonate in your soul. Oh friend, how I want to hear God say to me *Stony, you are my child, in whom I am well pleased. Stony, you are my son, in whom I am well pleased. Stony, you are my servant, in whom I am well pleased.*

What an honor it will be for God to say that about me: that He's pleased with me, that He's delighted in me. Don't you want that for yourself? Fellow believer, God delights in His friends. God is pleased with His friends.

God is not only pleased with His friends; He also loves to bless those who He calls His friends. He loves to bless those who He calls His family. He loves to bless those who He calls His children, and we're going to see that in a story from the book of 2 Chronicles. In this story, the king of Judah, King Jehoshaphat, who reigned from 870-849 B.C., faced a battle he was certain to lose, looking at the practical situation on the ground. The Ammonites and the Moabites had put their vast forces together and sought to crush King Jehoshaphat and the kingdom of Judah. King Jehoshaphat knew he had no hope for victory on his own. He knew he needed divine help to prevail. He humbly sought the Lord's help as he called his

Friend Of God

nation to prayer. As he stood in front of his people in the House of the Lord, he proclaimed these words in a cry to the Lord:

6 *"O Lord God of our fathers, are You not God in heaven, and do You not rule over all the kingdoms of the nations, and in Your hand is there not power and might, so that no one is able to withstand You?*

7 *Are You not our God, who drove out the inhabitants of this land before Your people Israel, and gave it to the descendants of Abraham Your friend forever?*

8 *And they dwell in it, and have built You a sanctuary in it for Your name, saying,*

9 *'If disaster comes upon us—sword, judgment, pestilence, or famine—we will stand before this temple and in Your presence (for Your name is in this temple), and cry out to You in our affliction, and You will hear and save.'*

10 *And now, here are the people of Ammon, Moab, and Mount Seir—whom You would not let Israel invade when they came out of the land of Egypt, but they turned from them and did not destroy them—*

11 *here they are, rewarding us by coming to throw us out of Your possession which You have given us to inherit.*

12 *O our God, will You not judge them? For we have no power against this great multitude that is coming against us; nor do we know what to do, but our eyes are upon You."*

This was King Jehoshaphat praying to God, asking God, *'God, we stand before you. We have a battle in front of us. We don't know how to win this battle. Are you not the God who gave your descendants this land, the descendants of Abraham, your friend, your son?* He was mentioning the fact that God had blessed the descendants of Abraham, who God called His friend. He was reminding God of the fact that the people of Judah were still the apple of God's eyes. He was reminding God of His promises, knowing that the Lord wouldn't turn His back on His chosen children if they turned to Him in the time of their trouble. He reminded God about their father, Abraham. Why was he able to do that? It was because Jehoshaphat was a friend of God, but it was also because Abraham was a true friend of God to whom God had made promises.

God loves to bless His friends. He loves it when we remind Him of His promises to us. He wants to shower His love and blessings on us. He doesn't just want to bless His friends with prosperity all around. He wants to bless them with the best blessing they can receive in His presence because His presence is everything. His presence means everything.

In (Exodus 33), Moses was having a conversation with the Lord God almighty. The context was the children of Israel sinning greatly against God by worshipping a golden calf that they had made in order to worship it. The Lord was going to punish them greatly, but Moses pleaded with the Lord not to punish them as their sins demanded. Even further, He asked that the Lord should have His presence go with Israel as they left the desert to go towards the Promised Land. This was a big ask from Moses, given what the children of Israel had just done in worshipping an image they had built with their own hands. They had broken God's law by making graven images and even further bowing down to worship the lifeless calf they had made.

The Lord said to Moses these words: "*I will also do this thing that you have spoken; for you have found grace in My sight, and I know you by name.*" The New International Version puts it this way: "*I will do the very thing you have asked, because I am pleased with you and I know you by name.*" The Living Bible writes it thus: "*Yes, I will do what you have asked, for you have certainly found favor with me, and you are my friend.*" The Message Bible translates it in this manner: "*All right. Just as you say; this also I will do, for I know you well and you are special to me. I know you by name.*"

The Lord God Himself referred to the special place that Moses had in His heart. Moses was such a friend to the Lord that God was very pleased with him. God was answering Moses' request simply because Moses had found grace or favor in God's sight. This is what it means to be a friend of God. God blessed the children of Israel with His abiding presence simply because Moses, whom God looked favorably on, asked for it. If you are a friend of God, it means that God can bring a revival to your city simply because you have found favor in His sight. You can be the reason why God decides to start an awakening in your nation. You could be the reason why God brings about a spiritual revolution in your geographical territory. You could be the reason why the Lord breaks the demonic stronghold over your land.

Earlier, we had seen how, in the midst of God's displeasure at the human race, Noah found grace and favor in the sight of God. The same thing happened with Moses. This time around, God's anger was not at the whole world but at His own chosen people. God told Moses He would do what Moses asked only because Moses was a dear friend to Him. He knew Moses by name. He was basically saying Moses was a dear friend of His. God decided to reward the nation of Israel with His presence because of Moses, His friend and

God Is Pleased With His Friends

faithful servant. God wants to bless His friends with His presence.

God wants to answer your prayers like He answered the prayers of Moses. God answered the prayer of Moses because Moses was a friend of God. Amen. (Psalm 147:11) says, "The *Lord delights in those who fear him, who put their hope in his unfailing love.*" The Lord takes pleasure in those who honor Him and trust in His unwavering goodness, kindness, and mercy. I want that to just sink into your spirit. If you honor God, He delights in you. He wants to take pleasure in you. He wants you to find grace in His sight. He wants to know your name. How lovely and amazing it'll be for me to know that my God, my Creator, my King, my Savior, my Redeemer knows my name.

There is a song that Israel and New Breed, the gospel music group, sang many years ago. The words of the song are:

I have a Maker
He Formed My Heart
Before even time began
My life was in hands

He knows my name
He knows my every thought
He sees each tear that falls
And hears me when I call

I have a father
He calls me his own
He'll never leave me
No matter where I go

Friend Of God

He knows my name
He knows my every thought
He sees each tear that falls
And hears me when I call.[1]

Friend, I have a friend who knows my name. I have a friend who hears me when I call. I have a friend who sees every tear that falls out from my eyes. I have a friend that's closer than a brother. I have Jesus. I have God as my friend.

Are you a friend of God? Are you a friend of the Almighty God? Does He look at you and say, *Hadassah or whatever your name is, is my daughter, in whom I am well pleased?* Does God look at you that way? What an honor it is to be loved by God, and for God to delight in me, and for me to have found grace in the sight of the Lord.

If you are not a friend of God today, well, here's another opportunity for you. Look to the heavens. Look to the Lord and say, '*God, I have sinned. I'm a sinner. Forgive me of my sins. Wash me clean in your blood. Save me, Lord Jesus. May I become part of the testimony of your greatness and your salvation. Save me, Lord. Wash me and cleanse me with your blood. Fill me with your Holy Spirit so I can be born again. May I be saved by the blood of Jesus. I believe that Jesus Christ came to die on the cross for me to set me free from my bondage of sin, hell, and the grave. Hallelujah. I am victorious through the salvation that Christ has brought for me. Not that anything I have is of my doing. I have nothing to boast of. It's all been by your grace and mercy towards me. Thank you, Lord. Amen.*'

I want to be a friend of God, one whom He is pleased with. One who has found grace and favor in His eyes. One who is special to Him. Do you want to also?

Chapter 5

God's Friends Are Friends Of Other Believers

"And let us be concerned about one another, and be stirring up one another unto love and good works; Not forsaking the assembling of ourselves together, even as some are accustomed to do; but rather, encouraging one another, and all the more as you see the day drawing near."
(Hebrews 10:25-26 A Faithful Version).

A friend of God is friends with other Christian believers. The scriptures command us to be friendly and likeminded with other believers. We are to be with other believers of like mind. The words in the verses above from the Book of Hebrews ought to light a fire in our hearts. The Message translation beautifully puts those verses in this manner: *Let's see how inventive we can be in encouraging love and helping out, not avoiding worshiping together as some do but spurring each other on, especially as we see the big Day approaching.*

Right here, we see a clarion call for believers to always gather together with one another. This is the reason why we have Sunday services in churches all around the world. This is why we have times of worship and fellowship between believers and Christians in different forms, functions, and capacities in churches and fellowships.

Friend Of God

All around the world, from Asia to Sub-Saharan Africa, from North America to South America, and from Australia to Europe, there are millions of people calling on the name of the Lord together in communion with other believers. They sing and pray in communion with other Christians and with other friends of God. I love the melodious Hillsong praise song, *People Just Like Us*. The lyrics read:

> *'All over the world, people just like us*
> *Are calling Your Name*
> *And living in Your love*
> *All over the world, people just like us*
> *Are following Jesus"*[1]

Let the message of that song sink in for a second. Friends, the gathering of saints, wherever we find ourselves all around the world, is a very beautiful sight that we can't help but cherish, but even more than a beautiful sight, it is also a command from the Lord.

Gathering together as a community to worship and fellowship is not just some tradition. It's not just something the old church fathers came up with as a good idea. No, we are encouraged in scripture to come together with other believers and other Christians. There is something powerful about several people from different families, different races, different creeds, different cultures, and different societal backgrounds coming together to worship God. What a delight it is to see believers coming together to commune with each other, coming together to fellowship with one another. There is something beautiful about that.

Our theme scripture for this chapter implores us not to forsake the assembly of the brethren. We are to strive to keep the company of other members of God's big and beautiful family. We ought to be inventive in encouraging and loving fellow believers, and helping others out, and to not avoid worshipping together.

There are two elements to the Christian faith. There is the private element, which deals with the relationship between you and God. That element is the foundation of your faith in Christ. I call this the vertical element of Christianity. Jesus died on a wooden cross that points in all four directions. One side of the cross is vertical, and the other side is horizontal.

The vertical element of the cross deals with our relationship that looks heavenward. This describes our relationship with God Almighty. Jesus came first and foremost to restore that broken relationship between God and man. We all, ought to have a personal relationship that exists between us as individuals and God.

But there is another element that I call the horizontal side of the cross. This part of the cross speaks to the relationship God wants us to have with our fellow man. The Christian faith is, first and foremost, relational in regard to the Lord. However, there is also a corporate component of our faith. God doesn't want you isolated. God wants you in friendship with other like-minded children of His. The enemy likes to isolate us. You need God-appointed friends in your life who will help catch you when you fall. Even the great man of God, Moses needed Aaron and Hur to hold up his hands, when they needed to be held up in order to allow the Israelites to win a battle (Exodus 17:12-14). The Puritan preacher, Thomas Brooks said *"Let those be thy choicest companions who have made Christ their chief companion"*.[2]

Friend Of God

God doesn't want you to avoid worship with your fellow believers. God doesn't want you to avoid worship with your fellow Christian friends. I want you to not forget this. If you forget anything you read in this chapter, don't forget this: God is very pleased when He looks down on the earth and sees His friends and children, Christians or believers, being in harmony with other children of His. When we do this, we bring glory and honor to God. God is so pleased at such a sight. His manifest presence can show up anywhere fellow friends and children of His decide to come together to worship and lift up His holy name and, in so doing, also edify one another.

We were not made to live this life on our own. God created us for companionship and friendship. J Vernon McGee said, *"There is a brotherhood within the body of believers. And the Lord Jesus is the Common Denominator. Friendship and Fellowship Are the Legal tender among believers"*.[3]

Yes, God doesn't want His children or friends to be lonely. He is so pleased at the sight of His children coming together and gathering in harmony. Now, if you know that God is so pleased with that sight, would you not want to work towards ensuring that there are such moments where believers come together, commune with each other, and love one another, but also worship God at the same time? Our Lord and God is pleased at such a sight. He looks down from His holy heaven and says, 'I am pleased with my children.' Just the mere thought of our Lord being so approving of such a sight makes me want to do everything I can to ensure it keeps happening.

Let's read another scripture that gives us further insight into this idea. (1 Corinthians 1:10) says, *"Now I plead with you,*

God's Friends Are Friends Of Other Believers

brethren, by the name of our Lord Jesus Christ, that you all speak the same thing, and that there be no divisions among you, but that you be perfectly joined together in the same mind and in the same judgment."

For a moment, settle your mind on the phrase, *'Now I plead with you.'* This is the Apostle Paul earnestly entreating believers to do what is commanded. It's almost like he's begging you about what he is about to instruct you on. In a sense of deep concern and importance for what he is about to say, he employs the name of our Lord in his earnest plea. What, then, is this earnest plea? It is that you will speak the same thing and that *there be no divisions among you, but that you be perfectly joined together in the same mind and in the same judgment.*

The foremost apostle has one desire, and that is to see the body of Christ be together as one. This is Paul the Apostle pleading with you in the name of the Lord Jesus saying, 'Be of one mind, be friends, be together.' Friends, we lack unity in the body of Christ, and God hates that. Christ wants us to be unified under the banner of His name. His desire has always been that we would be one (John 17:21). Our Lord has always wanted us to someday come to the unity of the faith. That is the picture of the spotless and unblemished bride for whom He is coming back.

In a narration of what the first Christians did, (Acts 2:42) reads thus: *"All the believers devoted themselves to the apostles' teaching, and to fellowship, and to sharing in meals (including the Lord's Supper), and to prayer."* The believers of the early church spent time in the doctrine of the apostles, which we now know as the word of God, and fellowship with one another in the breaking of bread.

The Contemporary English Version put it this way: *"They spent their time learning from the apostles, and they were like family to each other. They also broke bread and prayed together."* It further reads: *"Then fear came upon every soul for many wonders and signs were done through the apostles. Now, all who believed were together and had all things in common and sold their possession and goods and divided them among all as anyone had need. So, continuing daily with one accord, one accord, friendship with other friends of God in the temple and breaking bread from house to house. They ate their food with gladness and simplicity of heart, praising God and having favor with all the people and the Lord added to the church daily those who were being saved."* (Acts 2:43-47).

There is a reason why the holy sacrament of Holy Communion that we do in remembrance of the Lord is referred to as communion. In other words, it is not just about eating the bread and wine in a manner that reminds you of Christ. It is also a sacrament done in fellowship with other believers.

What an example for us to follow. The preceding verses describe what the early church did, and that is what God still wants us to keep doing. Do you have Christian friends in your life? Do you have true friends of God who are also your friends? A friend of God is friends with other friends of God. A friend of God is friends with other believers. A friend of God is friends with other children of God. God wants a communal feeling amongst His children. He's pleased at the sight of unity. The Bible says in (Psalms 133:1), "How *good and pleasant it is for brothers to dwell together in unity."* God wants you to develop and maintain friendships with other friends of God who have a mind for the Lord as you do. He wants you to live in friendship with other believers and develop that communal feeling you receive when assembling together. God is calling you to a higher place, and in that higher place that He's calling you to, it's not just going to be you. There are other believers; there are other children of God, and there are other friends of God, and guess what? A friend of God will be a friend of his or her fellow Christian brothers and sisters. Amen.

In Ephesians, we are implored to *"behave in a manner worthy of the calling you have received, with all humility, gentleness, and patience, bearing with one another in a spirit of love. Make every possible effort to preserve the unity of the Spirit through the bond of peace. There is one body and one Spirit, as well as one hope to which you have been called by your vocation, one Lord, one faith, one baptism, one God and Father of all, who is over all and through all and in all."* (Ephesians 4:1-6).

The Apostle Peter beseeches us, saying, *"Finally, all of you be like-minded [united in spirit], sympathetic, brotherly, kindhearted [courteous and compassionate toward each other as members of one household], and humble in spirit."* (1 Peter 3:8, AMP).

While in prison, Paul stirs up the church by saying, '*Fulfill my joy by being like-minded, having the same love, being of one accord, of one mind. Let nothing be done through selfish ambition or conceit, but in lowliness of mind let each esteem others better than himself. Let each of you look out not only for his own interests, but also for the interests of others."* (Philippians 2:2-4).

The proof that we love the Lord is found in our love for our fellow Christians. I don't know how certain Christians can read verses like these above and still insist on dividing the church. The rise of social media and platform growth tactics like using clickbait content to generate views has led to an excessive amount of vitriol in the Christian community. The videos that seem to get the most views are those that are focused on attacking or tearing down another believer. Certain so-called social media discernment ministries that spend their time tearing down others for their own selfish benefits have arisen. What I see in the church today is sad and alarming. What we do to each other devolves into downright nasty and vitriolic interactions. This, my friends, is not pleasing to the eyes of the Lord. The Lord doesn't seek uniformity from us; He seeks the unity of the faith.

We cannot be uniform as a church; seeking that would be a utopian goal. All across the body of Christ, there exists amazing and exciting diversity. The way Africans tend to praise the Lord seems more exuberant and louder than the way folks here in the West do. One church might be all about the old hymns, another, contemporary worship, and another, Gregorian chants. The flavor doesn't matter, and all the various styles of worship reflected in Christ's church across the earth give us a glimpse of what heaven will be like, a place where men and women from every tribe and tongue will be gathered together, praising the Lord for endless generations. God doesn't seek uniformity from us, but He desires that we be united in truth and in our love for Him, which is reflected in our love for one another.

I love Jesus, but I don't love the church.

All too often, I hear people say, *Oh, I love Jesus, but I don't love the church*. Ummm… no, sir, that is not how this works. The church, the ekklēsia, is the body of Christ. You may have a problem with man-made structures and traditions, but the church is intrinsically not a regular institution. It is the body of Christ, which He shed His blood and paid a ransom for.

God's Friends Are Friends Of Other Believers

The church of Christ is very precious to the heart of God. You can say *I don't like certain things in the church, but I love the church*. Think about it this way. I see certain churches marry themselves too closely with certain politicians that carry out policies antithetical to the teachings of Christ. I get a little mad about it, but I don't jump to condemning them because of that one instance. What I choose to do instead (*I fail to do it sometimes when I give heed to my flesh*) is pray for them. That should be the course of the believer whenever we see something in the church that doesn't sit right with the Spirit of God in us. Our first course of action should be to get down on our knees and appeal to the Head of the church (Christ) who sits in heaven and hears our every cry. It is His church, after all, and He knows what is best for it. You might think you know the best course of action for addressing such ill or trespass. Well, friend, we don't know what is best. Our Lord in heaven knows what is best.

Maybe all that is needed to fix that issue is for someone to get on their knees and intercede for that brother or sister in Christ. Maybe all that is needed is someone praying and standing in the gap for that church or Christian organization so that the agenda of Satan does not prevail in that situation.

As a friend of God who loves the Lord and His church, that should be your first course of action. Before you send out that sinister or rude comment, PRAY! Before you get mad and frustrated at what you are seeing, PRAY! Before you clench your fists in wrath and complain to your friends and family, PRAY! As a friend of God, your greatest weapon for any task is prayer.

That is one reason why I am very cautious about throwing condemning words about denominations, preachers, or Christian entities, whether they be churches, schools, charities, or foundations. Except if what they pronounce and stand by is blatantly anti-biblical or anti-Christ, I wait to judge. I want to give Christians the benefit of the doubt. Maybe it was a poorly worded line in a sermon or interview on TV. I am not looking for any Christian to be perfect. The Law of Love commands me to believe all things (1 Corinthians 13:7). To believe all things means to give others the benefit of the doubt. Our knee-jerk response should not be to think of the worst, especially when it concerns our fellow brethren. The goal is to walk worthy of our Lord, be imitators of Him, and downright examples of His kingdom here on earth.

When Jesus sensed that the enemy had taken hold of Peter, He did not instantly condemn him and send him to the wolves. He did not cast him aside. Rather, he said to him, *"Simon, Simon! Indeed, Satan has asked for you, that he may sift you as wheat. But I have prayed for you, that your faith should not fail; and when you have returned to Me, strengthen your brethren."* (Luke 22:31-32). For a moment, pause and compare the response that Jesus had and the response that we Christians seem to give today. Isn't it very different? Jesus' response was to pray for His disciples. Our response typically today is to jump into a furor and castigate the church and whoever we deem the new enemy. Rather than castigate and criticize, PRAY!

Chapter 6

God's Friends Are Not Ashamed Of God

"He would be a strange friend that never crossed your threshold if you could help it; that was evidently uncomfortable in your presence, and ill at ease till he got away from you, and that when he came was struck dumb, and had not a word to say for himself, and did not know or feel that he and you had any interests or subjects in common."
- Alexander Maclaren

God's friends are not ashamed of God. Let's read from (Matthew 10:32-33). Jesus said, *"Therefore whoever confesses Me before men, him I will also confess before My Father who is in heaven. But whoever denies Me before men, him I will also deny before My Father who is in heaven."*

No true friend of God will ever be ashamed of their identity as a friend of God. Are you truly a good friend of someone if you are afraid of publicly identifying with them? If you can only be friends with someone when nobody's watching, you are truly not their friend. If you can only be a friend of someone when nobody else is there to see you guys bond together, then you are no true friend.

A true friend stands with their friends in times of distress. True friends stick with their friends through thick and thin. I am not talking about fair-weather friends. I am talking about a true friend. True friends will always stick by you no matter

Friend Of God

what you are dealing with. They will do so in times when everybody wants to turn against you. If you have a true friend, you can be sure that they will always vouch for you. You can be sure they will say, I'm *going to speak good about you. You know what? I'm going to talk favorably about you. You know what? I'm going to represent you, right? I am going to stand in and say, I am proud to call you a friend.*

The question I have for you is, 'Are you that way with God? Are you that way with the Lord Jesus on your social media? Are you afraid of ever talking about God? I'm not saying that every single day, you should go out there and post and bombard people with scriptures and all of that stuff. But from a heart perspective, are you ashamed of your Savior? Are you ashamed of the One you call your best friend? Are you ashamed of the One you call a friend that sticketh closer than a brother? If God is truly your friend, if you are truly in an intimate relationship with God, you ought not to be ashamed of Him. You're supposed to be bold about Him. Jonathan Edwards said, *"True boldness for Christ transcends all, it is indifference to the displeasure of either friends or foes. Boldness enables Christians to forsake all rather than Christ, and to prefer to offend all rather than to offend Him"*.[2]

You're supposed to be able to represent Him everywhere you go. Jesus says, if you deny Me before your friends and your family here on earth, I will deny you before My Father in heaven. He was saying that there's no point to our friendship if you deny Me. You've got to be able to stand and represent your friendship with the Lord Jesus Christ.

Let's read another scripture, shall we? In (Psalms 34:1-2), King David talking about his friendship with the Lord, declares, '*I will bless the Lord at all times; His praise shall continually be in my mouth. My soul shall make its boast in the Lord; The humble shall hear of it and be glad.*'

David was declaring that the praises of God were going to be on his lips continually, both in public and in private. He was declaring that he would bless the Lord at all times, in all seasons, and in every situation, he found himself in. David wanted the humble and afflicted to hear him as he gave praises to God. He goes on to declare that his soul will boast in the Lord. He wanted the afflicted to hear and rejoice. What will the afflicted hear from David's mouth? They'll hear of his boasting in the Lord.

Do you boast in God all day long so others can look and rejoice? Do you boast in the Lord continually so that others can look and praise God, your Father in heaven? Or do you only boast of yourself and what you have, and your possessions, and your abilities, and your talents, and the things you think make you great? How about you be a man after God's heart like David was and boast in the Lord?

In his letter to the Corinthians, the apostle Paul reemphasizes this notion. In (2 Corinthians 10:17), he states what we ought to boast about. He writes, "*Let the one who boasts boast in the Lord.*" We who call ourselves Christians or friends of God are not to boast about ourselves, but we are to boast about the Lord. In verse 18, he goes on to remind us why we ought to boast only in the Lord. '*For it is not the one who commends himself who is approved, but the one whom the Lord commends.*'

Let those words sink into your spirit for a minute. When you boast in the Lord, you show that you are proud and not ashamed of being identified as a friend of God. What an honor it is to be identified as God's friend. It is the greatest honor of all. No accolade on this earth remotely compares to it. You cannot be ashamed of the Lord. You cannot be ashamed of the God that you call your friend. Hallelujah.

David once again declares in (Psalm 20:7 NIV) that *'Some trust in chariots and some trust in horses, but we trust in the name of the Lord our God.'* Another version says some boast in chariots, and some boast in horses, but we will boast in the name of the Lord our God. In today's terms, chariots and horses speak of your wealth. It refers to your abilities and possessions. It refers to all the connections that you have. It speaks to all the influence that you have. Do you boast in what you think makes you great, or do you boast in the Lord?

The writer of the Book of Hebrews declares, *'Both the one who makes people holy and those who are made holy are of the same family. So, Jesus is not ashamed to call them brothers and sisters. He says,*

"I will declare your name to my brothers and sisters; in the assembly I will sing your praises." (Hebrews 2:11-12 NIV).

Jesus is not ashamed to call you and His brothers and sisters. He is not ashamed of calling you His friend. If your Lord and Savior Jesus Christ is not ashamed to call you a friend of His, then why should you be ashamed to boast in Him and to boast about Him? Why are you ashamed of telling others that you are His friend? God's friends are not ashamed of God. God's friends are not ashamed of the Lord's name. If you are ashamed of the Lord, then it's time for a diagnostic check on your spiritual life because God's friends are never ashamed of the Lord God of Israel.

God's Friends Are Not Ashamed Of God

Daniel was a true friend of God. The scriptures say he had an excellent spirit in him and, therefore, excelled in everything he did. He was so successful that King Darius planned to have him installed as the governor of his realm. The other satraps and administrators who did not serve the Lord were not happy about this and sought to find anything they could use against Daniel to prevent his ascent. They tried and could not find any fault in him, and they concluded that they could attack him through his public expression of worship to God. In a conceited manner, they proposed a law to the king that stipulated that anyone who prayed to any deity or entity other than the king for the space of a month should be thrown into a pit where lions could devour them.

They knew that according to the customs of the Achaemenid Persian Empire, any law that was made by the king could not be overturned, even by the king himself. The proposal was made a law and Daniel's enemies waited and watched to see Daniel defy this law as they knew about his devotion to his God. Daniel, of course, being a friend and servant of the Most High God, did not care one bit. For Daniel, his friendship and devotion to God was the most important thing. He didn't care about what the king would think. He didn't care about this highly sought-after position the king had been considering him for. He didn't think about the risk of being eaten by lions or devoured by those vicious beasts, for the mistake of worshiping God was a badge of pride and honor to him.

His foes saw it as the ultimate weapon to bring him down. Daniel saw it as just an opportunity to lay his life down for his cherished Lord and King. A friend of God like Daniel is so sold out to the Lord that their safety and life become second thoughts when it has to do with the worship of the King of kings. Daniel was never going to shy away from identifying with his maker.

The apostle Paul also lived his life with this same approach. In his letter to the Philippians, he says:

"Indeed, I count everything as loss because of the surpassing worth of knowing Christ Jesus my Lord. For his sake I have suffered the loss of all things and count them as rubbish, in order that I may gain Christ and be found in him, not having a righteousness of my own that comes from the law, but that which comes through faith in Christ, the righteousness from God that depends on faith that I may know him and the power of his resurrection, and may share his sufferings, becoming like him in his death." (Phil 3:8-10).

It alarms me that there are many Christians who will proudly wear their favorite sports team merchandise but shriek at any public association with their Lord and Savior, Jesus Christ. Some Christians will not hesitate to talk about their favorite celebrity, movie, TV show, or hobbies but find it inconvenient to talk about the Savior of their souls.

For many Christians, the approval of man has become more important than the approval of God. I am not saying you have to be the guy who always wears a Jesus t-shirt and has Christian stickers on their automobile vehicles (*I tend to be one*). We all have our ways that we show our affinity, and love for our Lord. However, a friend of God should never shy about expressing their love for the Lord. You don't have to be aggressive and off-putting in your approach. In fact, I would advise that you do it in moderation, but always ask yourself if you are representing your Lord with your life and with your decisions.

God's Friends Are Not Ashamed Of God

The scripture enjoins us *to 'always be ready to give a defense to everyone who asks you a reason for the hope that is in you, with meekness and fear.'* (1 Peter 3:15). Someone once sang, *'You can have all this world; give me Jesus.'* Oh, how I pray that those words become the heart cry of those who call themselves Christians.

Why are friends of God not ashamed of Christ and His gospel? We are not afraid because we know whom we are friends with. We recognize that He is the creator of the heavens and the earth. We know He is all-knowing and all-powerful and that He is the all-sufficient God. We know He is the Way, The Truth, and the Life. We know He is our kinsman Redeemer. We know He is our everything.

How can we be ashamed of the One who gave His life for us? How can we be ashamed of the One who took the broken pieces of our lives and put them back together? How can we be ashamed of our Way maker, Miracle worker, and Promise Keeper? How can we deny the Author of our faith and the Bishop of our souls? How can we deny the one who adopted us even though we were wretched and good-for-nothing people? How can we be ashamed of the Lily of the Valleys, the Rose of Sharon, and the Ancient of Days? How can we be ashamed of the King of Glory? How can I be ashamed of Ebenezer, my stone of help? How do you expect me to be ashamed of my Rock of Refuge and my hiding place? No, I will not be ashamed of the One who, despite His divinity gave His life for me. God's true friends will never be ashamed of God.

Chapter 7

God's Friends Are Not Friends Of The World

"You adulterers! Don't you realize that friendship with the world makes you an enemy of God? I say it again: If you want to be a friend of the world, you make yourself an enemy of God."
- (James 4:4 NLT).

In the verse above, James expresses a very clear statement. As he writes to believers, he wonders why this message has not sunk in already. The reason why such a clear message can be difficult to accept and internalize is because of how easy it is to be a friend of the world. That, however, should not take our eyes off this reminder. James was implying *Do you not know that someone who desires friendship with the world desires hostility to God*. The original word used there is enmity. You can call it animosity, hostility, or discord. Enmity with God is the opposite of friendship with God. Being a friend of the world means that you are now standing as an enemy of God.

You cannot be a friend of the world and, at the same time, be a friend of God. It doesn't work that way. My fellow Christian, it simply doesn't work that way. The great preacher, D.L Moody said, *"If I walk with the world, I can't walk with God."*[1]

Oh, child of God, whoever wants to be a friend of the world makes himself an enemy of God. James, in the 5th verse of the 5th chapter, goes on to say, *"Or do you think that the*

God's Friends Are Not Friends Of The World

Scripture says in vain, "The Spirit who dwells in us yearns jealously"? Friends, the God we serve is a jealous God. He wants you for Himself. He does not want to share you with somebody else. He wants you for Himself. He wants your heart. He wants your soul. He wants your spirit. He wants your mind. He wants everything about you. He wants the totality of your being. The Bible says, *"You shall love the Lord your God with all your heart, with all your soul, and with all your strength."* (Deuteronomy 6:5).

You don't get to serve God with one part of you. You don't split yourself into compartments, giving one part to the world, one part to other things and people, and one part to God. Either your life is all about Jesus, or it's about Jesus having no place in your life. He is either everything or He is nothing. You don't get to do some Jesus. You don't get to do some of the Lord. You get to do all of Jesus. It's all of Him or nothing at all.

When a man seeks friendship with God, he must understand that God's interests have to become his own interests. God's friends delight in pleasing the Lord and doing His will. God wants you to go beyond subservient obedience. He wants to mold your heart and mind to reflect His. Only then, can you truly be called a friend of God. A gospel writer once said you cannot love the Lord your God and the things of this world at the same time, and in the same way, you cannot love your sin and love God together. It doesn't work that way. It is okay to have a liking for things. It is not okay to love things if you say you love God and want to be known as His friend. You can like some of the pleasures of this life. There is a difference between the word *love* and the word *like*. It's okay to like money, but it's not okay to love money. To love something is to become driven by it, right? It's okay if you like taking a trip to a vacation destination. It is okay to have a good time celebrating with family and friends. It is okay to like having fast cars and designer shoes. God will never hold that against you.

In his remarkable commentary, Charles Ellicott writes, *"Renunciation of the world, in the Christian promise, is not forsaking it when tired and clogged with its delights, but the earliest severance from it; to break this vow, or not to have made it, is to belong to the foes of God, and not merely to be out of covenant with Him. The forces of good and evil divide the land so sharply that there is no debatable ground, nor even halting-place between. And if God be just, so also is He jealous"*.[2]

When the scripture tells us not to love the world, it is saying don't give your full devotion to those things. When you like something, it means you have an interest in doing it, but you can live without it. It is okay to want to have something. It is not okay to desire to pursue something, no matter the cost to your life, family, integrity, and relationship with God. When you love something or someone, you offer your full and total devotion to them. That's why the only people we're supposed to love like the Lord are our spouses. That's why the Bible says, *husbands love your wives as Christ loves the church*. Our love for the Lord becomes our model of love for the man or woman that God has given to us to spend our lifetime on earth with. That's how a marriage becomes successful. If a husband loves his wife, as Jesus Christ has loved His church, He obeys God's commands and, in so doing, shows his love for the Lord.

I ask again: Do you want to be a friend of God? Well, if you do, it is time to say goodbye to the world, the things of

God's Friends Are Not Friends Of The World

this world, and the people of this world because they will not stand for you. They don't like God. They don't like the things of God. Therefore, you ought to have nothing in common with the world. This may be a hard saying, but it is true. We see this as an instruction in (Romans chapter 12:2), which says, *"And do not be conformed to this world, but be transformed by the renewing of your mind, that you may prove what is that good and acceptable and perfect will of God."*

The New Living Translation puts it this way: "Don't *copy the behavior and customs of this world, but let God transform you into a new person by changing the way you think. Then you will learn to know God's will for you, which is good and pleasing and perfect."* 19th-century theologian and preacher, Albert Barnes said, *"The "friendship of the world" is the love of that world; of the maxims which govern it, the principles which reign there, the ends that are sought, the amusements and gratifications which characterize it as distinguished from the church of God. It consists in setting our hearts on those things; in conforming to them; in making them the object of our pursuit."*[3]

Jesus told us about how the world will see those who want to be known as friends of God. In (John 15:18-21), He said,

18 *"If the world hates you, you know that it hated Me before it hated you.*

19 *If you were of the world, the world would love its own. Yet because you are not of the world, but I chose you out of the world, therefore the world hates you.*

20 *Remember the word that I said to you, 'A servant is not greater than his master.' If they persecuted Me, they will also persecute you. If they kept My word, they will keep yours also.* **21** *But all these things they*

Friend Of God

will do to you for My name's sake, because they do not know Him who sent Me."

Do not be surprised when people who live with a carnal or ungodly mindset do not care about you one bit. Don't be astonished when people in places of government, culture, and great influence do not like what you have to say.

This may sound a little political, but don't be surprised when most of Hollywood hates you. They may even use derogatory terms to describe you. They will call you the crazies of the Bible belt or Bible fundamentalists. They may call you a Bible-thumping redneck and even mock you for acting the way you do. They may falsely deride you for acting like you are the one who knows God the best or the best Christian in the nation. When you hear such words, don't be surprised. (1 John 3:13) says, *"Do not marvel, my brethren, if the world hates you."* Friends, don't be surprised when they mock you and laugh, saying, *'Your God is not real. He is all fiction. He is just a product of your imagination. You are deceiving yourself following the commands of an obsolete 2000-year-old book that's not meant for the 21st century."*

When you hear these things, scripture says, do not be surprised.

Don't be surprised when Hollywood and the elites in society mock and deride you for your beliefs. After all, you cannot love the world and God at the same time. In (1 John 2:15), we are commanded thus: *"Do not love the world or the things in the world. If anyone loves the world, the love of the Father is not in him."* That is very self-explanatory, and I don't even think I need to expand on that further. If you love the world, the love of the Father is not in you. If you are a friend to the world, there is no way you are going to be a friend to God. It cannot work. They're not going to all of a sudden love you. Why? They don't love God. Because they hate God and the things of God, they will hate you. Don't be surprised, oh Christian. Don't be perplexed.

(1 John 3:1) says, *'Behold what manner of love the Father has bestowed on us, that we should be called children of God! Therefore, the world does not know us, because it did not know Him.'* As our Lord is, so we are, and we will be treated the same way our Lord was treated. The reason why the world does not know us is that it did not know Him. That's the reason why the world does not love you or your beliefs. They look down on your beliefs. They mock you; they mock your beliefs. They do that to you because they also did not love Jesus, who was sent to die on the cross for their sake.

The apostle Paul describes the things of God and the things of the cross as foolishness to those who are of the world. Think about it for a second. The things of God seem to be foolishness to those who don't believe. The concept of Christianity is total foolishness to them. You just have to look at atheistic, agnostic, and humanistic Reddit and Quora threads online to see how those outside the faith view Christianity. They think we are delusional and brainwashed. The things of God will not make any sense to them because they do not have the heart of the Father. They don't have the spirit of God living in them. They don't know what it means to walk with God, and they have never had a true encounter with Jesus. Oh, friends, we're privileged to have known God!

So, don't be surprised when they mock you, look down on you, or deride you for your beliefs. Don't be surprised when social media giants try to suppress and stifle your freedom of speech. Don't be astonished when they seek to prevent you from saying things that are righteous and true and holy. Don't be surprised when they hate you for holding your ground and staying true to your beliefs.

As I write this, a young 20-year-old soccer player on the U.S. Women's Soccer National team has been forced to apologize for making statements true to the word of God on social media. Every day in our mainstream media, we see a campaign to silence anything that speaks of God or Jesus. Recently, in Canada, there was an uproar in the NHL over a player, Ivan Provorov, who declined participation in the celebration of LGBTQ+ pride. Think about that for a second. He was derided because he declined participation in an event that would be in opposition to the values of his faith. In response, he was bashed, and there were lots of calls on major sports media to have kicked away from the league. They wanted him to bow to their agenda and for refusing to do so, they came after him. This happened in our so-called free Western society. I praise God Ivan did not back down. He understood the mission and knew that to be a friend of God meant you would and could be seen as an enemy of the world.

In the opening ceremony of the 2024 Olympics, the government of France and the Olympics organizing committee mocked the Lord by having drag queens pose as Jesus and His disciples in a subtle reenactment, of the famous painting of the Lord's Supper. They didn't care about the optics and possible pushback for such a blasphemous act. When confronted by the outcries of the Faithful, they decided to lie and say they were reenacting the party painting of the Greek god, Dionysius. Of course, social media posts made by participants in that grotesque act of debauchery confirmed

God's Friends Are Not Friends Of The World

what Christians had asserted about the mockery of Christ. This is what the world is like, my friends. They don't love God and our Christ, and without the light of the gospel penetrating their hearts, they will sit and love the darkness that they are in. They did not love or care for Jesus, and so they will likely not love you or care for you. You have been set apart by the Lord your God. Act like you've been set apart. Let the world's hatred of you for your faith become a badge of pride for you. Don't be afraid when they throw stones your way. Revel in the fact that you are favored by the only person that truly matters. You are a friend of God, so you are favored by God.

Chapter 8

A Friend Of God Walks With God.

I come to the garden alone,
While the dew is still on the roses,
And the voice I hear falling on my ear,
The Son of God discloses...

And He walks with me, and He talks with me,
And He tells me I am His own,
And the joy we share as we tarry there,
None other, has ever, known![1]
- The Song, In the Garden

In (Genesis 5:22-24), we are introduced to a man called Enoch. We don't know much about Enoch, but the little said about him in the book of Genesis actually reveals a lot about the type of relationship he had with God. It says Enoch walked with God, and then he was no more because God took him away. So, when it says *He was no more*, it's speaking of the fact that he was translated to heaven without dying physically on the earth. Enoch walked with God and then he was *no more*. Friends of God walk with God.

What does it mean to walk with God? To walk with God means to have daily fellowship with Him, daily communion with Him. Leonard Ravenhill said, "*Smart men walked on the moon, daring men walked on the ocean floor, but wise men walk with God*".[2]

A Friend Of God Walks With God.

Let us compare how a few other translations present (Genesis 5:24) as I think you will receive a deeper revelation of the concept of walking with God.

The Amplified Version says, *'And [in reverent fear and obedience] Enoch walked with God; and he was not [found among men], because God took him [away to be home with Him].'*

The Voice translation says, *'but Enoch had such a close and intimate relationship with God that one day he just vanished—God took him.'*

The Classic Amplified Bible Version says, *'And Enoch walked [in habitual fellowship] with God; and he was not, for God took him [home with Him].'*

The Living Bible says he was *'in constant touch with God, he disappeared, for God took him!'*

The Easy English Bible says, *'Enoch lived to please God all this time, then Enoch was not there anymore. God took Enoch to be with him.'*

The Good News Translation says, *'He spent his life in fellowship with God, and then he disappeared because God took him away.'*

The International Standard Version describes it as Enoch spending the totality of his life *'communing with God—and then he was there no longer because God had taken him.'*

The Message Bible says, *'Enoch walked steadily with God. And then one day he was simply gone: God took him.'*

The New International Version says, *'Enoch walked faithfully with God; then he was no more because God took him away.'*

Friend Of God

The New Living Translation says Enoch was *'walking in close fellowship with God. Then one day, he disappeared, because God took him.'*

In spite of what translation, you might prefer, it is clear that the verse speaks of a faithful, consistent, and intimate walk of fellowship with God. His journey started so well with the Lord, and therefore there was not even a need for him to be translated through death. It just got to the point where God was like, 'I enjoy your friendship so much, and so I am going to allow you to skip death; an event that is appointed for every man.

Wow, doesn't that bring chills down your spine? Can you imagine God being as pleased with you as His friend that He has you skip the appointment that every mortal has with death? I may not get to skip death, but I want to have such fervent and continual fellowship with God as Enoch did. I want to be called a friend of God who is full of faith. Ask yourself, am I walking with the Lord as I should? Or, how is my walk with the Lord? What does my relationship with the Lord look like?

The Book of Hebrews describes Enoch's relationship with the Lord in this way: "*By faith Enoch was taken away so that he did not see death, "and was not found, because God had taken him"; for before he was taken he had this testimony, that he pleased God. But without faith it is impossible to please Him, for he who comes to God must believe that He is, and that He is a rewarder of those who diligently seek Him."* (Hebrews 11:5-6.).

As a friend of God, he had a testimony: he pleased God. Wow, what a remarkable statement to describe a man. I long

A Friend Of God Walks With God.

for that to be my testimony also: that I was a friend of God who pleased the Lord. He was a man of faith and belief, and the totality of his faith and confidence was in God. What a powerful testimony.

Enoch walked with God by faith. He had confidence that the God He served was more real than the air he was breathing. Jim Cymbala, who I love said, *"Faith is content just knowing that God's promise cannot fail. This, in fact, is the excitement of walking with God"*.[3]

Like Enoch, we ought to be close to God if we want to be called friends of God. A friend of God doesn't just keep God at bay. A friend of God doesn't just keep God on the side as they say, 'You know what? I'm going to get to you, God, when I need you. I'm going to only come to you calling for help when I need you, and when I need you to answer my prayer.

No, no, no. A friend of God understands the ways of God because they walk with God. They understand how God works. They understand the deeds of God. They understand the heart of God. Why? Because they continually chase after God. They continually seek after God. They continually thirst for God. They continually desire God. They want to be in constant, consistent fellowship with God. They wake up in the morning, and they desire the Lord. They go to bed at night and desire God because they want to walk with God. They want to have a continuous, consistent, constant relationship with their Maker.

Jesus said, *'Blessed are those who hunger and thirst for righteousness, for they shall be filled.'* (Matthew 5:6).

Friend Of God

Enoch was a friend of God because he walked side by side with God. Because of Jesus and what He did on the cross, we, too, can walk with God. So, my question to you is, how is your walk with the Lord? Do you want to call yourself a friend of God? How is your walk with the Lord?

Let's look at another scripture. (1 John 1:3) says, *'That which we have seen and heard we declare to you, that you also may have fellowship with us; and truly our fellowship is with the Father and with His Son Jesus Christ.'*

See, John was trying to say that this is what it is like to walk with God. What is it? It's to have fellowship with God, the Father, and His Son, Jesus Christ. To the apostle John, fellowship and friendship meant to be in constant communion with God. In our prayers, my wife and I conclude with praying (2 Corinthians 13:14), which says, *'May the grace of our Lord Jesus Christ, the love of God and the sweet fellowship of the Holy Spirit rest and abide with us now and forevermore.'* God wants us to be in constant communion and fellowship with Him. God wants us to walk continually with Him. Are you walking with the Lord?

A friend of God walks with God. In the Psalms, we see the heart of the psalmist who desired and longed for the Lord. (Psalm 42:1-2) says, *'As the deer pants for the water brooks, so pants my soul for You, O God. My soul thirsts for God, for the living God. When shall I come and appear before God?'*

This is the heart of a man who walks with God, desiring God as the famished deer in search of streams of water. They know they can't live without water, so they're constantly searching for water. That's how my soul longs for and deeply desires the Lord.

A Friend Of God Walks With God.

What does it mean for a soul to thirst for God? I've got a glass of water here with me as I write these words. What state would you be in if you've not had water in two to three days and you suddenly saw a glass of water around you? What will your reaction be? Well, I think I have an idea. You're going to thirst for it, and when you drink that full glass of water, you will no longer be famished.

In the same way that a thirsty man who hasn't had any water to drink in three days doesn't hesitate to drink that full glass, so we ought to desire our God. So, that means if you've not spent one or two days with the Lord and are a friend of God, something ought to stir up within you. If you're truly a friend of God, you're going to start panting for the heart of the Lord the same way your body causes you to pant for water when thirsty. You will desire the Lord if you've not spent time with Him in a day or a couple of days. You will begin to say, *'When can I go and meet with God? When can I go and fellowship with God? When can God and I have a talk? When can God and I have a moment of fellowship together?*

A friend of God walks with God. They desire God. They seek after the heart of God. They thirst for the Lord, their Maker and King. Does your heart desire God? Do you seek after God? Do you search for the deeper things of the Holy and Living Spirit of God? I am reminded of the worship song by Keith Staten called *Lord I Thirst for You*. The words read thus:

Lord I thirst for You
And I long to be in Your presence

Friend Of God

My soul will wait on You
Father draw me nearer
Draw me nearer
To the beauty of Your holiness.[4]

Does the antenna of your heart scan the frequency airwaves of the heavens and earth, looking for the companionship of the Lord? Do you say, '*God, I want to hear your voice. God, I want to know your ways. God, I want to be taught by you. God, I want to receive the revelation of your word. Holy Spirit, I want you to teach me how to live my life. I want you to order my steps. I want you to direct my day. I want you to straighten my path.*'

Does your heart seek for the Lord in such a manner? If it does, you are a friend of God. If it doesn't, you're not truly God's friend. My desire and heart cry is that you seek to be such a friend of the Almighty God today.

R.T. Kendall said, "*To know and enjoy God is the very essence of life. This is what we were made for, and apart from God we cannot attain our true end or purpose. In friendship with God, we find rest for our souls*".[5] One of the most beautiful worship songs I have ever heard is *To You* by Hillsong Worship. The words of this song speak of the heart of one seeking God's face and heart. It was released many years ago, in 2001, and here are the words:

Here I stand forever in
Your mighty hand
Living with Your promise
Written on my heart
I am Yours
Surrendered wholly to You

A Friend Of God Walks With God.

You set me in Your family
Calling me Your own
Now that I
I belong to You
Lord I need
Your Spirit Your Word Your truth
Hear my cry my deep desire
To Know You more
In Your name
I will lift my hands
To the King
This anthem of praise I bring
Heaven knows
I long to love You
With all I am
I belong to You.[6]

A blog writer said, "*Being in relationship with God is experiencing the presence of God in our private walk. A relationship with the Lord is all of the above with the addition of a sweetness that is indescribable. It is willing submission because we want to follow Him and be near Him. It is truly an intimate relationship that cannot be mimicked or faked or taken away*".[7]

To walk with God is to spend time with Him. It's also to treasure the time spent with God. You have to know God for yourself. Francis Howgill remarked that "*People substitute tradition for the living experience of the love of God. They talk and think as though walking with God was attained by walking in the footsteps of people who walked with God*".[8] Reading about others who have walked with God alone is not going to help you. You have to develop your own personal relationship with your Heavenly

Friend Of God

Father. A friend of God walks with the Living God. Do not ever forget that. I'll end this chapter with this quote from Eli Stanley Jones: *"To talk with God, no breath is lost. Talk on! To walk with God, no strength is lost. Walk on! To wait on God, no time is lost. Wait on!"*.[9]

Chapter 9

God's Friends Love His Presence

"One thing have I asked of the Lord, that will I seek after: that I may dwell in the house of the Lord all the days of my life, to gaze upon the beauty of the Lord and to inquire in his temple."
- (Psalm 27:4 ESV).

Of all the things in this world to seek after, David decided that the one thing he would constantly ask for and seek was to dwell in the presence of the Lord. The words in the verse above are the words of someone who is truly in love with God. Those are the words of someone who is truly God's friend, someone who is after God's own heart.

In the 8th verse of that chapter, David would go on to say, *'My heart tells me to pray. I am eager to see your face.'* Oh, friend how I long for a time when every child of God would cultivate a similar desire for God's presence as David did. What a role model for being a friend of God who valued the presence of God above everything else. David loved to encounter God's manifest presence.

The Power of His Manifest Presence

Friend, God's manifest presence is everything. It changes you and you are never the same again. It is life-giving and heart-transforming. His presence is Heaven touching Earth. A.W Tozer said, *"When the eyes of the soul looking out meet the eyes of God looking in, heaven has begun right here on this earth"*[1]. You may ask, what is this manifest presence of God you speak about? We know God to be omnipresent in that He is present everywhere at all times. There is nothing that escapes God, and there is nothing that He doesn't see or know. He is all-powerful (omnipotent), all-knowing (omniscient), and all-present (omnipresent). God's omnipresence is His all-encompassing and all-pervading presence. It is God's omnipresence that Jonah tried to escape from but couldn't. It is the presence spoken about by David when he said:

> *7 "Where can I go from Your Spirit?*
> *Or where can I flee from Your presence?*
> *8 If I ascend into heaven, You are there;*
> *If I make my bed in hell, behold, You are there.*
> *9 If I take the wings of the morning,*
> *And dwell in the uttermost parts of the sea,*
> *10 Even there Your hand shall lead me,*
> *And Your right hand shall hold me.*
> *11 If I say, "Surely the darkness shall fall on me,"*
> *Even the night shall be light about me;*
> *12 Indeed, the darkness shall not hide from You,*
> *But the night shines as the day;*
> *The darkness and the light are both alike to You."*

In spite of this, however, there exists a difference between God's manifest presence and His omnipresence. God doesn't show up in His manifest presence at all times, as we see when we talk about His omnipresence. He chooses certain moments to make Himself more real so you can feel a change in the atmosphere.

God's Friends Love His Presence

In His manifest presence, His profound glory and heavenly majesty are seen and experienced. His omnipresence is seen in places that are holy and unholy; however, His manifest presence only appears in a holy place; hence the command to Moses to take off your sandals, for the ground you stand on is holy ground (Exodus 3:5).

The appearance of God's manifest presence is seen throughout scripture. In Genesis, we read about how God would come down to the Garden of Eden to talk with Adam. That is an example of His manifest presence showing up. It is tangible and real. When God shows up in His manifest presence, it is unique and very apparent. You find the glory of God revealed when God shows up in this manner.

While Jacob lay down to rest one night, he had a dream where God appeared to him, revealing Himself as the God of his fathers. God also promised to be with Jacob wherever He went. When Jacob woke up from that dream, he declared, *"Surely the Lord is in this place, and I did not know it." And he was afraid and said, "How awesome is this place! This is none other than the house of God, and this is the gate of heaven!"* (Genesis 28:16-17). He would go on to call that place where he encountered the God of Heaven and Earth Bēth'ēl, which means house of God or a place of worship.

In (Genesis 32), we saw God's manifest presence again when this same Jacob wrestled with God all through the night.

It was God's manifest presence that Moses sought when he said to the Lord, *Show Me Your Glory*. Isaiah encountered God's manifest presence when he had a heavenly vision of God (Isaiah 6). It was the manifest presence of God that was spoken of when the people of Beth Shemesh (1 Samuel 6:20) said, *"Who can stand in the presence of the Lord, this holy God? To whom will the ark go up from here?"*

It was the manifest presence of God that Moses experienced in the burning bush, where God told him to *"…take off your shoes, for you are standing on holy ground"* (Exodus 3:5).

It is the manifest presence that is spoken of when Paul said, *"Now the Lord is the Spirit; and where the Spirit of the Lord is, there is liberty."* (2 Corinthians 3:17). It was the manifest presence of God that David was speaking about in his michtam when he said, *"You will show me the path of life; In Your presence is fullness of joy; At Your right hand are pleasures forevermore."* (Psalm 16:11).

It was the manifest presence of God that showed up as God's people praised and worshipped His holy name in (2 Chronicles 5:13-14):

11 *"And it came to pass when the priests came out of the Most Holy Place (for all the priests who were present had sanctified themselves, without keeping to their divisions),*

12 *and the Levites who were the singers, all those of Asaph and Heman and Jeduthun, with their sons and their brethren, stood at the east end of the altar, clothed in white linen, having cymbals, stringed instruments, and harps, and with them one hundred and twenty priests sounding with trumpets*

13 *indeed it came to pass, when the trumpeters and singers were as one, to make one sound to be heard in praising and thanking the Lord,*

God's Friends Love His Presence

and when they lifted up their voice with the trumpets and cymbals and instruments of music, and praised the Lord, saying:

"For He is good,

For His mercy endures forever,"

that the house, the house of the Lord, was filled with a cloud,

14 *so that the priests could not continue ministering because of the cloud; for the glory of the Lord filled the house of God."*

Wow, what a mind-baffling sight that would have been for God's presence and glory to be so strong that the priests and Levites could not go on with their tasks because God's glory and manifest presence were so real and tangible.

It was the manifest presence of God that showed up on the day of Pentecost when the 120 believers in the upper room got filled with the Holy Spirit as they obeyed Jesus, who had instructed them to tarry in expectation of the gift of the Holy Spirit. The scriptures say, *"When the Day of Pentecost had fully come, they were all with one accord in one place. And suddenly there came a sound from heaven, as of a rushing mighty wind, and it filled the whole house where they were sitting. Then there appeared to them divided tongues, as of fire, and one sat upon each of them. And they were all filled with the Holy Spirit and began to speak with other tongues, as the Spirit gave them utterance."* (Acts 2:1-4).

One of the most powerful episodes of God showing up in the might of His glory is found in (Exodus 19). This is how the Bible narrates it:

16 *"Then it came to pass on the third day, in the morning, that there were thunderings and lightnings, and a thick cloud on the mountain;*

and the sound of the trumpet was very loud, so that all the people who were in the camp trembled.

17 And Moses brought the people out of the camp to meet with God, and they stood at the foot of the mountain.

18 Now Mount Sinai was completely in smoke, because the Lord descended upon it in fire. Its smoke ascended like the smoke of a furnace, and the whole mountain quaked greatly.

19 And when the blast of the trumpet sounded long and became louder and louder, Moses spoke, and God answered him by voice.

20 Then the Lord came down upon Mount Sinai, on the top of the mountain. And the Lord called Moses to the top of the mountain, and Moses went up.

21 And the Lord said to Moses, "Go down and warn the people, lest they break through to gaze at the Lord, and many of them perish.

22 Also let the priests who come near the Lord consecrate themselves, lest the Lord break out against them."

23 But Moses said to the Lord, "The people cannot come up to Mount Sinai; for You warned us, saying, 'Set bounds around the mountain and consecrate it.'"

24 Then the Lord said to him, "Away! Get down and then come up, you and Aaron with you. But do not let the priests and the people break through to come up to the Lord, lest He break out against them."

25 So Moses went down to the people and spoke to them."

In the simplest terms, you can basically say that the manifest presence of God is revealed when God shows up in a real and tangible way.

God's Friends Love His Presence

Although David wrote the majority of the psalms in scripture, there were other psalms written by other people who also loved God's presence. A beautiful Psalm in scripture is one written by the sons of Korah. These were men who also deeply loved the presence of God, as evidenced by their words in Psalm 84. Friend, you will not hear words more beautiful than this that speak of one's desire for the presence of our Almighty God. Here are those exhilarating words:

> *1 "How lovely is Your tabernacle,*
> *O Lord of hosts!*
> *2 My soul longs, yes, even faints*
> *For the courts of the Lord;*
> *My heart and my flesh cry out for the living God.*
> *3 Even the sparrow has found a home,*
> *And the swallow a nest for herself,*
> *Where she may lay her young—*
> *Even Your altars, O Lord of hosts,*
> *My King and my God.*
> *4 Blessed are those who dwell in Your house;*
> *They will still be praising You. Selah*
> *5 Blessed is the man whose strength is in You,*
> *Whose heart is set on pilgrimage.*
> *6 As they pass through the Valley of Baca,*
> *They make it a spring;*
> *The rain also covers it with pools.*
> *7 They go from strength to strength;*
> *Each one appears before God in Zion.*
> *8 O Lord God of hosts, hear my prayer;*
> *Give ear, O God of Jacob! Selah*
> *9 O God, behold our shield,*
> *And look upon the face of Your anointed.*

Friend Of God

10 *For a day in Your courts is better than a*
thousand.
I would rather be a doorkeeper in the house of my
God
Than dwell in the tents of wickedness.
11 *For the Lord God is a sun and shield;*
The Lord will give grace and glory;
No good thing will He withhold
From those who walk uprightly.
12 *O Lord of hosts,*
Blessed is the man who trusts in You!"

Oh, friend, is one day in the presence of the Lord worth more to you than a thousand days elsewhere? Would you rather be a poor slave doorkeeper in the house of the Lord than a wealthy business mogul? Do you desire the presence of the Lord so much that it becomes the air you breathe? Are you desperate for the endearing touch and voice of your king? Do you long for the Lord to wrap His arms around you daily in His warm embrace? An esteemed writer once said, "*No human heart I a millionth part so sweet, and so capable of satisfying you as God's*".[2]

Can you be like the songwriter that sang:

This is the air I breathe
This is the air I breathe
Your holy presence living in me
This is my daily bread
This is my daily bread
Your very word spoken to me
And I'm desperate for you
And I'm lost without you.[3]

God's Friends Love His Presence

God's friends are people of praise and worship.

A.W. Tozer said, *"I can safely say, on the authority of all that is revealed in the Word of God, that any man or woman on this earth who is bored and turned off by worship is not ready for heaven"*.[4] God's friends derive joy in praising and worshipping God. It is their happy place. Nothing brings more excitement to a friend of God than lifting up the name of Jesus. Oh, child of God! You were created to sing praises to the Most High God. God's friends understand that God is exalted and enthroned on the praises of His people.

The Psalmist speaking of the Lord says, '*Yet you are holy, enthroned on the praises of Israel*' (Psalm 22:3). Friends pause and think about that for a second. God, the creator of Heaven, and Earth, is enthroned on our praises. God is delighted when we praise Him. Nothing gives the Lord more pleasure than when His people lift up their voices and hands in praise and adoration of His majestic name. Sincere, Spirit-led praise and worship is the key to experiencing the manifest presence of God.

A friend of God understands the power of praise and worship and how an atmosphere of God-exalting praise and worship brings about the manifest presence of the Living God. Friends, it is in the presence of God that we find our ultimate joy and purpose. God created you for His pleasure, and you will only find your true life's purpose in worshiping Him. The psalmist said, *"You make known to me the path of life; in your presence there is fullness of joy; at your right hand are pleasures forevermore."* (Psalm 16:11). God's friends highly value the manifest presence of God.

Friend Of God

When Paul and Silas were bound in chains in jail, they didn't spend their time there whining and complaining about God abandoning them. They didn't murmur, asking God why He had allowed them to be thrown into jail. Instead, the scriptures say, *'But at midnight Paul and Silas were praying and singing hymns to God, and the prisoners were listening to them. Suddenly there was a great earthquake, so that the foundations of the prison were shaken; and immediately all the doors were opened and everyone's chains were loosed.'* (Acts 16:25-26).

They could have spent their midnight hours being angry and mad. However, these men were true friends of God. They quickly got to doing what they knew to do best: praising, worshiping, and praying to God. They sang hymns of praise, and God responded in kind: He sent His manifest presence into that jail cell. It was so heavy that, as seen in the verse above, there was an earthquake, and the prison doors were open. Friends, Paul and Silas valued the manifest presence of God, and they were people of praise and worship. Choose to be a man or woman of praise and worship because God's friends revel in giving glory to God.

Changed by His presence

Friends, once you catch a glimpse of the glory of God, you are forever changed. God's presence truly makes all the difference. His friends understand what His presence means, and they cherish it dearly. The scriptures declare, *'Blessed is the one you choose and bring near, to dwell in your courts! We shall be satisfied with the goodness of your house, the holiness of your temple!"* (Psalm 65:4 ESV). Spending time in God's presence will make you more like Jesus Christ. Harry Emerson Fosdick beautifully stated that *"The steady discipline of intimate friendship with Jesus results in men becoming like Him"*.[6]

How to encounter God's Manifest Presence

Now, you may say, but Stony, I haven't encountered the manifest presence of God as you have talked about. Friend, the key to the manifest presence of God is very simple: Seek Him with all your heart. There are no tricks or gimmicks involved. You get to know someone by spending time with them. If you don't spend time with someone, you will never get to know them. Time spent together is an intimacy created. If you seek the Lord without reservation and all of your heart, He will make Himself known to you. We have a certain and sure promise from God that states thus: *"When you seek me, you will find me, when you will seek me with all your heart."* (Jeremiah 29:13 EHV). It is that simple folks.

God is always present with His friends

God's friends know that the Lord is always with them because they know what it is like to be in communion with the King of kings and the Lord of Lords. They walk around with confidence in their heart and their heads held up high because the Alpha and Omega is always with them.

I am reminded of this verse that I prayed every day growing up: *"Even though I walk through the valley of the shadow of death, I will fear no evil, for you are with me; your rod and your staff, they comfort me."* (Psalm 23:4). The Holy Scriptures again declare, 'He *who dwells in the shelter of the Most High will abide in the shadow of the Almighty. I will say to the Lord, "My refuge and my fortress, my God, in whom I trust."* (Psalm 91:1-16 ESV).

Friend Of God

King David, who constantly sought after the heart of God, said, *'Therefore I will offer sacrifices of joy in His tabernacle; I will sing, yes, I will sing praises to the Lord.'* (Psalm 27:6). He knew perfectly what the presence of the Lord meant, and he cherished it above riches, wealth, or glory.

Moses was a friend of God who valued the presence of God, and God, in turn, declared to Moses, saying, *"My presence will go with you, and I will give you rest."* (Exodus 33:14 ESV).

Sitting at His Feet - What Matters Most.

38 *"Now it happened as they went that He entered a certain village; and a certain woman named Martha welcomed Him into her house.*

39 *And she had a sister called Mary, who also sat at Jesus' feet and heard His word.*

40 *But Martha was distracted with much serving, and she approached Him and said, "Lord, do You not care that my sister has left me to serve alone? Therefore, tell her to help me."*

41 *And Jesus answered and said to her, "Martha, Martha, you are worried and troubled about many things.*

42 *But one thing is needed, and Mary has chosen that good part, which will not be taken away from her."*

(Luke 10:38-42).

The story above conveys a powerful and timeless truth. The Lord cares more about your friendship with Him than what you do for Him. It is a good thing to serve the Lord. It is an admirable thing to work and labor for the kingdom of God, but it means nothing when you do all of that and forsake precious time spent in His presence. God desires an intimate walk with you and me.

He is calling for us to come up higher in our walk with Him. Your work for the ministry of the gospel and for the Lord is important, but what's much more important is your walk with Him. Much more important is the time you spend sitting at His feet and listening to what He has to say to you. The Lord has so much to teach us, more than our entire lifetime could provide time for.

We, however, like Martha, get caught up in doing the work of the Lord and serving needs out there and forget to make time for the thing that matters most: the good part that Mary chose. What Mary chose forms the heart of friendship with God and that is time with Jesus.

The presence of God gives us life and joy that we could get nowhere else. We get refreshed and rejuvenated in His presence. His presence is everything to me, and I implore you that it should be what you seek after above anything else. This is the true walk of the believer. This is what we are saved to experience. In Heaven, we will be in His manifest presence forever. God, however, doesn't want us to wait for heaven to encounter the glory of His presence. We can begin that experience right here on Earth if we seek Him with all of our hearts.

Friend, it is time to prioritize sitting at the feet of Jesus and just being in His presence. The presence of God means the world to those who are truly friends of God.

Chapter 10

God's Friends Speak To God, And They Listen To God

For prayer is nothing else than being on terms of friendship with God.
- Teresa of Avila

*"My sheep hear My voice, and I know them, and they follow Me. And I give them eternal life, and they shall never perish; neither shall anyone snatch them out of My hand." **(John 10:27-28)***

God's friends speak to God, and they listen to God. God's friends communicate with God. God's friends spend time communicating with God and being in fellowship with God. How do we do that? We do that through prayer and meditating on His Word and His promises, who He is, what He has done for us, and what He says He will do for us. Amen.

God's friends speak to God and God's friends listen to God. Shortly after the idolatrous rebellion of the Israelites and their worship of the golden calf in Exodus 32, we see the grace of God evident in Exodus 33. One episode in that chapter is pertinent and speaks volumes of God's desire to communicate with us, His children, just as we communicate with our fellow human friends. (Exodus 33:11) says, *'So the Lord spoke to Moses face to face, as a man speaks to his friend.'*

God's Friends Speak To God, And They Listen To God

Now pause for a second and let that sink in. God, the creator of the heavens and earth, spoke to Moses, His servant and friend, face to face as a man would speak to his friends. That, my friends, was a very unique aspect of the relationship that Moses enjoyed. What a privilege for any man to have such an audience with God where He speaks to him just like He spoke to Moses, face to face. They spoke to each other like they were friends to each other, which they were. They spoke to each other like you would speak to your spouse or you would speak to your family member. I can imagine one of their conversations probably went in this manner:

God: Hello Moses, how are you doing today? How is that hip? Oh, let me touch it right now and heal it completely. How are my people doing? How are the children of Israel doing? Have they been complaining again? Have they started lacking faith in me again?

And then Moses would give a report of what the children of Israel had done to the Lord. They would communicate. Moses would communicate with God about God's heart, and God would speak to Moses about his heart and what He had been dealing with him about.

Just like Moses, the Lord desires to show us His secrets. The Bible says, *"The secret of the Lord is with those who fear Him, and He will show them His covenant."* (Psalm 25:14). God's secrets are available to those He calls friends. An old preacher said: *There is a strange wisdom and insight, sometimes amounting even to prophetic anticipation, which creeps into a simple heart that is knit closely to God. But whether the result of our friendship with Him be such communication of such kinds of insight or no, we may be sure of this, that, if we trust Him, and love Him, and are frank with Him, He will in so far be frank with us, that He will impart unto us Himself, and in the knowledge of His love we shall find all the know.*

You see, friend, how I desire that you believe me when I say truthfully, God wants us to have a relationship, a friendship with Him as akin to a man speaking to his friend. Your Lord and God wants us to speak to Him, and He wants to speak to us. He wants us to hear His beautiful, amazing, powerful voice, and He longs to hear your voice, too.

Jesus is the Vehicle for the Father's Voice.

The writer of the Book of Hebrews starts out his wondrous book by saying:

1 *"Long ago God spoke many times and in many ways to our ancestors through the prophets.*

2 *And now in these final days, he has spoken to us through his Son. God promised everything to the Son as an inheritance, and through the Son he created the universe.*

3 *The Son radiates God's own glory and expresses the very character of God, and he sustains everything by the mighty power of his command. When he had cleansed us from our sins, he sat down in the place of honor at the right hand of the majestic God in heaven."* **(Hebrews 1:1-3 NLT).**

This scripture speaks to the idea that in the era of the Old Covenant or, as some of you may know it, the times of the Old Testament, God spoke to His people through oracles, prophets, seers, and judges.

He spoke to the children of Israel through Moses, as we saw in (Exodus chapter 33:11). He spoke to the children of

God's Friends Speak To God, And They Listen To God

Israel through Major Prophets like Isaiah, Ezekiel, and Jeremiah, and Minor Prophets like Nahum and Obadiah, Hosea, Zephaniah, and Zechariah. He spoke of repentance and judgment through fiery prophets like Elijah and Elisha. Prophets and judges like Samuel were outstanding as vessels of the Word of the Lord.

The Prophet Nathan was a vessel of the Lord to bring rebuke to great kings like King David. He was the prophet sent to rebuke David for committing the sins of adultery and murder.

Though He spoke through these great men of God in the past, scripture says that He no longer needs to use a prophet to speak to you. I'm not saying God does not speak through prophets to us today. I believe He still does, as there is nothing in scripture that says He will not before Jesus comes again.

Unlike many out there who want to convince you that the Lord doesn't speak in manifold ways as He did before, I encourage you to study and see if you can find anywhere in all of the Bible where it says the gifts of the Holy Spirit would cease after the first century. Don't let any man give you their own conclusions. Read the Word of God for yourself.

Hardline cessationism will try to silence the voice of God in your life. Cessationism (*The idea that the gifts of the Spirit completely ceased to exist after the Bible was fully compiled*) is a man-made idea that is not grounded in scripture and should be completely abandoned. My friends who espouse this theology may sound like they are speaking from scripture, but they aren't. In fact, the Apostle Paul actually encourages us time and time again to seek the gifts of the Holy Spirit (1

Friend Of God

Corinthians 14:1). The Bible affirms our ability to hear the voice of God, and that is very important.

I don't want to dwell on that point for too long as I believe it's a subject for another book. The point I am driving at, however, is that in this era of our Lord, God speaks to us through His only begotten Son, Jesus Christ, and through the Holy Spirit whom He has given to you. If you are a child of God, if you are born again, you've got the Holy Spirit living on the inside of you, and God wants to speak to you, through Jesus, His Son, and through the Holy Spirit whom Jesus promised to you. Jesus promised that He would send the Holy Spirit, who would be a helper and comforter to us.

God wants to speak to you. Oh, friend, do you want to be known as a friend of God? Well, if you do, how do you think you can be called His friend when you have no intimate communication with Him? How are you going to be a friend of God if you don't speak to God, and how are you going to be a friend of God if you don't hear God?

A major sign of your friendship with your earthly friend is that you speak to them and that you also hear from them. It is a two-way street. You listen, and you speak. It is the same thing with God. A friend of God speaks to God in prayer and then listens to God in prayer and meditation. Your daily communication with the Lord is so essential to your Christian walk. David, the prolific Psalmist in (Psalm 145:18-19) said *The Lord is near to all who call upon Him, to all who call upon Him in truth. He will fulfill the desire of those who fear Him; He also will hear their cry and save them."*

God's Friends Speak To God, And They Listen To God

Friend, the Lord is nearby. He's close to those who call upon His name in spirit and in truth. David was saying that the Lord's friends, those He is close to, are those who call upon Him. One of the main signs of friendship is that you know a lot about them, and they know a lot about you. When you talk about your best buddies, you can confidently say *that guy is my best buddy and he gets me. He understands me. She understands me. She gets me. We're friends. We spend time together. We talk to each other. We listen to each other. They listen to what I have to say. They're close to me. They really know me.*

These are all things we can say about someone who is truly close to us, someone we call a dear friend. You cannot truly know someone if you're not close to them; or if you're not near to them. The Lord is near to all those who call on him, those who call upon His name. The Bible says in (Genesis 4:26) that after Seth had borne a son, men began to call upon the name of the Lord, and this has never ceased since then. If you want to be close to God, if you want to be a friend of God, if you want to be near to the Lord, what do you do? You call upon the Lord, for it is those who call upon the Lord who are near to God.

(1 Peter 5:7 NIV) says, *'Cast all your anxiety on him because he cares for you.'* Another translation says, 'Casting all your worries. Others say, 'Casting all your cares on Him for He cares for you. Who do you cast all your worries and cares on? You cast it on the Lord Jesus because the Lord cares for you, oh friend.

The Lord God Almighty cares for you. Your friend, who is also your Lord and Savior, Jesus Christ, truly and deeply cares for you. He wants to deal with your worries. He wants to hear about the anxieties that you are struggling with. He wants to hear about your fears. He wants to hear your pain. He wants to hear about your heartache. He wants to hear about what you went through throughout your day. He wants to communicate with you. He wants you to speak to Him in prayer, but He also wants you to listen to what He has to say. He wants to comfort you. He wants to be your friend. He wants to be near you. He wants you to cast your anxieties and burdens on Him. Yes, He can handle all of it.

What is that thing that bugs you? What is that thing that worries you? What is that thing that keeps you awake at night? What is that thing that troubles you? What is that need? You are bothering yourself with something you can't solve on your own.

What is that puzzle that you can't seem to decipher? Your God, the Lord God Almighty, the creator of heaven and earth, wants to hear from you. He wants to hear about your worries, fears, and doubts. He wants to hear about your pain, your troubles, and your sorrows. He wants to hear about your joys and your days of happiness. He wants to hear from you on your highs and on your lows. He wants to be your friend, one who can be a listening ear.

He wants you to cast your anxieties on Him because He cares for you. Why does He care for you? He does because you are a friend of His. You are a friend of God. God's friends listen to God, and God's friends speak to God. They commune with God. They have daily fellowship with God. Do you want to be a friend of God? You've got to know that every day, you've got to be able to go to God in prayers with

God's Friends Speak To God, And They Listen To God

all your worries and your anxieties. Cast it on Him, but also, don't just talk, listen.

Don't be the one speaking the whole time in your moment of prayer. Take some time to listen, too. Take some time to be still. The Lord says to you today, *"Be still and know that I am God."* (Psalm 46:10). Have some quiet time in His presence. This is a time we call the hour of fellowship. Have some alone time with the Lord. Meditate on His Word. Listen to what He has to say to you for that day because it's in His words that you will receive peace and find victory. It's in His words that you will receive comfort for all of your troubles. It's in His Word that you will receive the joy and calmness you need in your heart to bring stillness to your storm.

You need the voice of the Lord. It is the voice that echoes over many waters. It is that powerful voice that is full of majesty. It is that glorious voice of the Lord that breaks the cedars and splinters the cedars of Lebanon. It is the voice that makes the mountains skip like a calf and a young wild ox. It is the voice that divides the flames of fire. It is the voice that shakes the wilderness.

Oh, friend, how I long to hear the voice of the Almighty God that soothes my soul. God's friends speak to God, and they listen to what He has to say. Just like you speak to your friends and you listen to what they have to say; God wants to do the same for you all believers. The Psalmist in (Psalms 85:8 AMP) said:

'I will listen [with expectancy] to what God the Lord will say, for He will speak peace to His people, to His saints (those who are in right

standing with Him)—but let them not turn again to [self-confident] folly'.

You might ask, Stony, what then are the ways that God speaks to us? Well, I am glad that I get to be able to write about that for you.

Ways God Speaks to His Friends

1. **His Word, the Bible:** The Holy Scriptures constitute the primary and most common way the Lord speaks to His children. The Psalmist said, '*Your word is a lamp to my feet and a light to my path.*' (Psalm 119:105). God's words are eternal and true. They are new every morning and never fall out of date. God's Word, as contained in the Bible, contains no expiration date since the scriptures say, '*The grass withers, the flower fades but the word of our God stands forever."* God's Word will accomplish all that has been said and written. '*So shall My Word be that goes forth from My mouth; It shall not return to Me[a]void, but it shall accomplish what I please, and it shall prosper in the thing for which I sent it. And a light to my path.*' (Psalm 55:11).

God's Word is inerrant, infallible, righteous, and true. His Word should be the definite and authoritative guide and standard for your life. God will never oppose what is written in His Word. The Lord is not frail, fickle, and ever-changing like us. In a fast-changing world, God's Word stands firm and ever true. When the ever-changing winds of this world blow by, don't get swayed by but stand firm on the unchanging Word of God.

God's Friends Speak To God, And They Listen To God

Whenever you pick up your Bible and begin to study its words, ask the Holy Spirit for help and guidance. Ask Him to teach you and reveal to you what you can't figure out for yourself, and I assure you that He will do just that. God's Word contains light, life, and truth that can't be overcome. The Apostle Paul writes that '*All Scripture is given by inspiration of God, and is profitable for doctrine, for reproof, for correction, for instruction in righteousness.*' (2 Timothy 3:16).

The enemy will always try to isolate you from friendship with God. One way he does that is to turn your eyes away from the truth of scripture. He wants you to doubt the Word of God. It is his oldest trick, and he still uses it today. The devil will try to convince you to doubt the truth and power of God's Word. The Lord Jesus prayed to God the Father, saying, '*Sanctify[a] them by Your truth. Your Word is truth.*' (John 17:17). (Proverbs 30:5) says, '*Every word of God is pure; He is a shield to those who put their trust in Him.*'

Do you want to draw closer to the Lord? Do you want to be a close friend of the Most High God? Do you seek true intimacy with the Father? Your starting point is to get into His Word. God's Word is your manual for friendship with God. It will tell you all that you need to know about the nature of God. Get that dusty Bible that has been sitting on your shelf for a while and dive deep into the sea of God's Word. Life-transforming treasures and secrets are found in God's Word.

So, friends, God's Word is eternal, and no matter how many times a man tries to extinguish it, it cannot be destroyed. Many emperors, kings, queens, and governments have tried to eradicate the Word of God, and all their attempts ended up in failure. Hang on to your Bible, child of God. It is the most powerful and precious book in all of history.

2. **Visions and Dreams:** We learn through the scriptures that God spoke frequently to His children and friends through visions and dreams. Many Muslims who come to know Jesus as Lord and Savior testify that they had dreams where Jesus revealed Himself to them. Those Muslims may have never believed the gospel just by hearing it from a random Christian out there, but they could not escape the very real and personal revelation of the Lord to them in a dream.

I know my mother to be someone whose dreams are accurate a lot of the time. Many dreams that she has dreamt have come to pass. It seems to be powerful that the Lord speaks to her in this way. I praise the Lord for that. Dreams and visions have always been used by God to send specific messages that He wants to send to different people and it is no different today. Here are a few instances where God spoke to people in scripture using visions and dreams.

➢ In (Genesis 15:1), God appeared to Abraham in a vision to remind Abraham of who He was and His covenant with Abraham: *"After these things the Word of the Lord came to Abram in a vision, saying, "Do not be afraid, Abram. I am your shield, your exceedingly great reward."*

➢ In (Genesis 20:1-7), God spoke to Abimelech in a dream warning Him not to touch Sarah as she was Abraham's wife: *"But God came to Abimelech in a dream by night, and said to him, "Indeed you are a dead man because of the woman whom you have taken, for she is [a]a man's wife." But Abimelech had not come near her; and he said, "Lord, will You slay a righteous nation also? Did he not say to me, 'She is my sister'? And she, even she herself said, 'He is my brother.' In the integrity of my heart and innocence of my hands I have done this." And God said to him in a dream, "Yes, I know that you did this in the integrity of your heart. For I also withheld you from sinning against Me; therefore, I did not let you touch her. Now therefore, restore the man's wife; for he is a prophet, and he will pray for you and you shall live. But if you do not restore her, know that you shall surely die, you and all who are yours."*

➢ In (Genesis 28:11-17), God appeared to Jacob, reminding Jacob that He was God and He would be with him and fulfill all that He had promised Jacob and his fathers, Abraham and Isaac:

11 *'So he came to a certain place and stayed there all night, because the sun had set. And he took one of the stones of that place and put it at his head, and he lay down in that place to sleep.*

12 *Then he dreamed, and behold, a ladder was set up on the earth, and its top reached to heaven; and there the angels of God were ascending and descending on it.*

13 *And behold, the Lord stood above it and said: "I am the Lord God of Abraham your father and the God of Isaac; the land on which you lie I will give to you and your descendants.*

14 *Also your descendants shall be as the dust of the earth; you shall spread abroad to the west and the east, to the north and the south; and in you and in your seed all the families of the earth shall be blessed.*

15 *Behold, I am with you and will keep[a] you wherever you go, and will bring you back to this land; for I will not leave you until I have done what I have spoken to you."*

16 *Then Jacob awoke from his sleep and said, "Surely the Lord is in this place, and I did not know it."*

17 *And he was afraid and said, "How awesome is this place! This is none other than the house of God, and this is the gate of heaven!"*

- In (Genesis 37:5-10), God revealed Joseph's future to him twice through dreams:

5 *"Now Joseph had a dream, and he told it to his brothers; and they hated him even more.*

6 *So he said to them, "Please hear this dream which I have dreamed:*

7 *There we were, binding sheaves in the field. Then behold, my sheaf arose and also stood upright; and indeed, your sheaves stood all around and bowed down to my sheaf."*

8 *And his brothers said to him, "Shall you indeed reign over us? Or shall you indeed have dominion over us?" So they hated him even more for his dreams and for his words.*

9 *Then he dreamed still another dream and told it to his brothers, and said, "Look, I have dreamed another dream. And this time, the sun, the moon, and the eleven stars bowed down to me."*

God's Friends Speak To God, And They Listen To God

10 *So he told it to his father and his brothers; and his father rebuked him and said to him, "What is this dream that you have dreamed? Shall your mother and I and your brothers indeed come to bow down to the earth before you?"*

➢ In (1 Kings 3:5 NIV), God appeared to King Solomon in a dream and asked Him for whatever His heart desired because Solomon loved the Lord: *"At Gibeon the Lord appeared to Solomon during the night in a dream, and God said, "Ask for whatever you want me to give you."*

➢ In the Book of Daniel, we see multiple visions that God gave to Daniel, who was also a friend of God.

➢ In the Book of Ezekiel, we see about 6 visions that the Prophet Ezekiel had.

➢ Jeremiah had visions from God, also.

➢ The Prophet Isaiah also had multiple visions from the Lord.

➢ In (Luke 1:11-22), an angel of the Lord appeared to Zachariah, an old priest, while he was in the temple to tell him that He would soon have a son who we know now as John the Baptist, who would prepare the way of the Lord Jesus.

➢ In the book of Matthew, an angel of the Lord famously appeared to Joseph, urging him not to divorce Mary after he found out that she was pregnant since the baby in her womb was conceived by the Holy Spirit. The angel of the Lord again appeared two more times to Joseph to flee to Egypt and also to return home from Egypt after it was safe to do so.

- In (Acts 10:1-6) an angel of the Lord appeared to a centurion named Cornelius and instructed him to send for Peter to come to his house and preach the gospel of Jesus to them. Through Peter's preaching, the whole house of Cornelius came to know Christ.

- The Apostle Paul received so many visions from the Lord throughout his ministry.

- The Apostle John the Beloved was certainly no stranger to visions, as one of his main writings, the Book of Revelations is made up mostly of visions the Lord showed him while he was on the island of Patmos.

These are only a handful of the many instances where God spoke to people through visions and dreams. As we walk through scriptures, we can see that our Sovereign Lord and God uses this medium to speak to people as He wills. Don't discount the Lord speaking to you in this manner because He can and He will.

3. **Inner Prompts in Your Spirit:** This is a common way that the Lord speaks to a lot of His children. These inner prompts are not audible voices but strong impressions in your spirit man. I have learned that the closer you walk with the Lord, the better your sensitivity to these inward promptings.

Sometimes, these prompts are to warn you from doing something you were planning on doing or going somewhere you had planned to go. These inner prompts could also be described as sensing things in your Spirit. It can also be described as being led by the Holy Spirit. These prompts from the Lord can come in different ways.

Sometimes, it happens through the Lord not giving you any peace about a certain thing, and sometimes, it could be affirmative in the Lord giving you full peace and comfort about a certain situation. To hear the Lord in this manner is truly life-changing, but I must stress that it is contingent on being sensitive to the leading of the Holy Spirit.

Have you ever felt led to pray for a certain person, nation, or even organization, and then later on, you found that your prayers were really important in bringing out the favorable outcome that the Lord nudged you about? Well, that is the prompting of the Holy Spirit.

In (Acts 15), the Early Church's council at Jerusalem sent a letter to the young Gentile believers at Antioch, Syria, and Cilicia. In the letter, they wrote to the Gentile believers telling them what they deemed was appropriate for Gentile believers and the unnecessary, burdensome demands that the Gentile believers didn't have to obey.

In that letter, the council and church in Jerusalem made this statement that is poignant for this subject matter: *It seemed good to the Holy Spirit and to us not to burden you with anything beyond the following requirements:* Note the words: '*It seemed good to the Holy Spirit and to us.*'

This was clearly not God speaking to them in an audible voice, or they wouldn't have used the word: *seemed*. It was an inner impression. It was a prompting by the Holy Spirit. Another example of God speaking through an inner prompting is in (Jude 3), which says, '*Beloved, while I was very diligent to write to you concerning our common salvation, I found it necessary to write to you exhorting you to contend earnestly for the faith which was once for all delivered to the saints'.*

Jude was planning on writing about an important topic – which was the salvation that Christ had brought to His children. I mean, the initial topic he was planning about was a very central Christian one, but the Lord had impressed on His heart a different topic to write about, which was more important for that moment.

4. **Through others, His vessels and other friends of God:** I tell you, friend, you are not the only one that God can speak to. He has several other people who hear from Him, too. He can speak through others regarding your life and situation. Don't dismiss what He has to say through others, especially if they are people you know love and serve the Lord in truth and integrity. It is, of course, important that you check what others say in comparison to what His Word, the Bible, says.

5. **The Counsel and Consensus of Righteous People:** This was how a lot of decisions in the Early Church were agreed upon. God would inspire righteous people to come to a consensus that He wanted. This is also reflected in an example I made earlier when talking about inner promptings from the Holy Spirit.

6. **Audible Voice:** This was a common way God spoke to people throughout scripture. With an audible voice, you can basically hear God like you would hear a regular person that you are having a conversation with.

God's Friends Speak To God, And They Listen To God

One of the clearest examples of God speaking through an audible voice is in the story of Samuel and how God called his name three times before while he served under Prophet Eli. We find that story in (1 Samuel 3).

1 *"The boy Samuel ministered before the Lord under Eli. In those days the Word of the Lord was rare; there were not many visions.*

2 *One night, Eli, whose eyes were becoming so weak that he could barely see, was lying down in his usual place.*

3 *The lamp of God had not yet gone out, and Samuel was lying down in the house of the Lord, where the ark of God was.*

4 *Then the Lord called Samuel.*

Samuel answered, "Here I am."

5 *And he ran to Eli and said, "Here I am; you called me."*

But Eli said, "I did not call; go back and lie down." So he went and lay down.

6 *Again the Lord called, "Samuel!" And Samuel got up and went to Eli and said, "Here I am; you called me." "My son," Eli said, "I did not call; go back and lie down."*

7 *Now Samuel did not yet know the Lord: The Word of the Lord had not yet been revealed to him.*

8 *A third time the Lord called, "Samuel!" And Samuel got up and went to Eli and said, "Here I am; you called me." Then Eli realized that the Lord was calling the boy.*

9 *So Eli told Samuel, "Go and lie down, and if he calls you, say, 'Speak, Lord, for your servant is listening.'" So, Samuel went and lay down in his place.*

10 *The Lord came and stood there, calling as at the other times, "Samuel! Samuel!" Then Samuel said, "Speak, for your servant is listening."*

Since this book is not exclusively about ways we can hear from God, I choose not to go in too deep on this mode of God speaking as it is also a very rare form of God speaking to His children. In my entire Christian life, which has been for most of my life, I believe I have only heard the audible voice of God once. It is rare, and so I will not impress it upon you to seek to hear His audible voice, as in God's sovereignty, He has chosen this as a rare form of communication with His children.

7. **Songs:** Have you been still, praying and meditating, and the right song that ministers to you in the right moment is brought to mind? Well, the Lord will sometimes use praise and worship songs to encourage and inspire us and even correct us. God can use anything, and He certainly will use the right songs at the right time to speak to you.

8. **Circumstances and Situations:** There are times when God will seek to get your attention, and He knows that the only way to get it is for you to face a difficult circumstance that causes you to pause and turn to Him. This has happened to me so many times. There are times when I know that I haven't walked in holiness as I should have or when I haven't made time

for Him as I should have, and the only thing that will get me to fall on my face and get on my knees is a circumstance that brings the automobile of my life to an emergency stop. Through circumstances and situations that we experience, God teaches us His children many lessons. Learn to perceive and obey the messages He is sending your way through circumstances that arise.

How You Can Start to Hear God's Voice Regularly as a Friend of God

1. Spend time in His presence in Worship and Prayer: This cannot be substituted for anything. There is no alternative.

2. Be humble and seek God's face.

3. Be willing and open to receiving from Him.

4. Spend time meditating on His Word.

5. When you pray, give yourself time to listen to the Lord in stillness.

6. Read God's Word out loud.

7. Be willing to receive what He is saying through other Godly people.

Chapter 11

God's Friends Lay Down Their Lives For God

*'Greater love has no one than this,
than to lay down one's
life for his friends.'* **(John 15:13).**

God's friends lay down their lives for God. You see, Jesus has to be our perfect example if we want to call ourselves friends of God. He is our ultimate model, and the utmost expression of friendship with God is the total sacrifice of one's life for God. Now, that may seem shocking to hear for some of you, given the spiritual food you may have been fed.

I am all for preaching God's Word in an encouraging and edifying manner. The Word of God is there to lift us up and lift our spirits up as we deal with the challenges of this life. I love to bring encouraging and uplifting messages to God's people and fully support the utility of those messages.

However, we cannot only exclusively focus on those elements of God's Word and not talk about the fact that, as true Christians, there are sacrifices we will have to make for our Lord. These sacrifices may be small for some, and others might pay bigger sacrifices, including laying down one's life for Christ. Some people might pay the ultimate price, which costs them their lives. We all have to sacrifice certain desires and pleasures in our walk with the Lord.

God's Friends Lay Down Their Lives For God

We know that the expression of someone laying down their lives for their friend was first exemplified by Jesus Himself, laying down His life on the cross of Calvary to save you and me. It was the ultimate expression of love. It was the greatest act of love anyone could give: giving up their life so that someone else could live. In giving up His life, even though He had no sin, He became our substitution; He became the propitiation for our sins and for the sins of the whole world. He took our place of shame and suffering so that we do not suffer but enjoy an eternal relationship with the Lord God Almighty, the Creator of the entire world.

Greater love, Jesus stated, *hath no man than this than for a man to lay his life down for his friends.* Now, let us turn that expression to ourselves. Greater love then hath no man than this, than for a man to lay down his life for his Lord. As a friend of God, your life is supposed to be sacrificed for Jesus and Jesus alone. This was the sentiment the Apostle Paul was expressing when he said, '*As for me, my life has already been poured out as an offering to God.*' (2 Timothy 4:6, NLT).

Now, how do we lay down our lives for the Lord? How do we sacrifice our lives for our God and King? Well, we're going to have the word of God tell us how we sacrifice our entire lives for the cause of our Lord and Savior, Jesus Christ, and for the cause of His gospel. What does it mean to sacrifice? What does it mean to give the ultimate prize? Now, the words from Jesus we are about to read are some of the strongest statements of His and He made many statements that seem radical to a whole host of people.

25 "*Now great multitudes went with Him. And He turned and said to them,*

Friend Of God

26 *"If anyone comes to Me and does not hate his father and mother, wife and children, brothers and sisters, yes, and his own life also, he cannot be My disciple.*

27 *And whoever does not bear his cross and come after Me cannot be My disciple.*

28 *For which of you, intending to build a tower, does not sit down first and count the cost, whether he has enough to finish it—*

29 *lest, after he has laid the foundation, and is not able to finish, all who see it begin to mock him,*

30 *saying, 'This man began to build and was not able to finish'?*

31 *Or what king, going to make war against another king, does not sit down first and consider whether he is able with ten thousand to meet him who comes against him with twenty thousand?*

32 *Or else, while the other is still a great way off, he sends a delegation and asks conditions of peace.*

33 *So likewise, whoever of you does not forsake all that he has cannot be My disciple."* **(Luke 14:25-33)**.

Now, if someone were to read those verses in the most literal sense, they may think of Jesus as some crazy nut for making such statements. They will wonder why this great teacher would have had His followers show hatred to their loved ones in order to fulfill the task of becoming His disciples.

Just reading at first sight, the words '*If anyone comes to Me and does not hate his father and mother, wife and children, brothers and sisters, yes, and his own life also, he cannot be My disciple* seem like an encouragement to committing fratricide in order to have the

God's Friends Lay Down Their Lives For God

honor of being Jesus' disciple. In the literal sense, that would be a commitment we would only expect of a narcissistic and domineering cult leader. Was Jesus asking you to be a mortal enemy of your family and friends in order to serve Him? Of course not! Jesus was saying, if you are going to be my disciple and if you're going to follow me, you have to make me such a priority that even your family seems like a distant thought when compared to me.

He was saying I have to become your everything, your all-consuming passion and desire. He was saying you have to kill yourself, not in a literal sense, but by putting your fleshly man to death. You have to die to self and live for me and me alone. You've got to sacrifice your old life for me. Now, that may seem like a tall order for someone at first, but when you realize all that He has done for you, such a request becomes very easy to take on.

You see, the great thing about our Lord is that even though He asks us to be willing to forsake all to follow Him, His burden and yoke, however, is easy. The life of faith is not one where you have got this giant stone around your neck and you are overburdened with this great demand on you. It is not religion as normal. It is a freeing demand that He places on you. In fact, what He asks to trade with you is so much lighter than the burden you already bear on your own.

One of my favorite words from our Lord was: '*Come to Me, all you who labor and are heavy laden, and I will give you rest. Take My yoke upon you and learn from Me, for I am gentle and lowly in heart, and you will find rest for your souls.*' (Matthew 11:28-29). The Message Bible puts it this way: "*Are you tired? Worn out? Burned out on religion? Come to me. Get away with me and you'll recover your life. I'll show you how to take a real rest. Walk with me and work with me—watch how I do it. Learn the unforced rhythms of grace. I won't lay anything heavy or ill-fitting on you. Keep company with me and you'll learn to live freely and lightly."*

Our Lord is not calling you to literally hate your family. In fact, He wants you to love them, as showing them love is actually a sign that you love God. What He is asking for is that He becomes the number one priority in your life. He is asking to be the center of your very existence. God doesn't want a spare room in your life. He wants all of you. That is what He demands, and your total surrender is the only way you can build a thriving friendship with Him. Is your life His to use as He sees fit? Are you totally surrendered? Can you say my life, my soul, all of it belongs to you?

The Shema prayer is the foundation of the Jewish faith. It has been that way since God uttered those words to His servant Moses thousands of years ago. In (Deuteronomy 6:4), God declared, *"Hear, O Israel: The Lord our God, the Lord is one! You shall love the Lord your God with all your heart, with all your soul, and with all your strength."* Jesus reaffirmed this declaration as the center of the Christian faith, too, in (Matthew 22:37), saying, *'You shall love the Lord your God with all your heart, with all your soul, and with all your mind'.*

You see, the call from God to love Him with all of your being is certainly not new. That has always been God's desire for His people: that they would love Him with the entirety of their being. Loving Him with everything you are is what laying your life down is about. It doesn't mean that every friend of God will be killed or martyred for following Jesus, even though that could happen. It means, however, that you are so sold out for God that even physical death for His sake means nothing since your life has already been poured out for Him.

A martyred Christian does not give their life for the Lord's sake the day they are physically killed. They laid down their lives for God the day they decided they would happily do that if it came down to that option.

In (Galatians 2:20), Paul said, '*I have been crucified with Christ; it is no longer I who live, but Christ lives in me; and the life which I now live in the flesh I live by faith in the Son of God, who loved me and gave Himself for me.*' He was still alive in the flesh when he made that statement, and yet he had decided to die to self. His life was Christ's to use as He saw fit. Charles Spurgeon expressed this sentiment in this way: "*We are dead with Christ, we are buried with Christ, we are risen with Christ; and there is no real spiritual life in this world except that which has come to us by the process of death, burial, and resurrection with Christ*".[1] Is your life that disposable to the Lord Jesus? David Brainerd said, "*As long as I see anything to be done for God, life is worth having; but O how vain and unworthy it is to live for any lower end*".[2]

When Jesus says, you have to hate your brother and mother and even yourself, He's saying, you've got to die to every one of those people and live for me alone. You've got to even die to yourself, to your will, and to your desires. That means He is not just to come first. He has to be everything to you. You've got to be dead to everything. You've got to hate everything. It's not as in hating them with hatred in your heart, no, but dying to them and allowing just Jesus Christ to be the centerpiece of your life. After Jesus becomes the centerpiece of your life, then other things can come in there, but He has to be the central and elevated focus of your life.

Friend Of God

When you say I have been crucified with Christ, you are saying I am dead to flesh. It is no longer I who lives anymore. Stony doesn't live anymore. Olivia doesn't live anymore. Burke doesn't live anymore. George doesn't live anymore. Kathy doesn't live anymore. Whoever you are doesn't exist anymore. It is Jesus Christ who lives now. Therefore, you can say *Jesus Christ lives in me and the life which I now live in, the flesh, I live by faith in the Son of God. My entire life now is all about Jesus. I'm dead to myself.* This is a radical call friend, but it is a radical call to be a friend of God. I'm dead. I'm dead.

Jesus understood this posture very well Himself while He was on the earth. In (John 4:34), Jesus said, *'My food is to do the will of Him who sent Me, and to finish His work.'* Laying down your life for God is doing the will of God, not your will. In the Garden of Gethsemane, He pondered on the cross that was set before Him. His disciple, Judas Iscariot, was about to betray Him. He was about to be separated from His beloved disciples whom He had done ministry with for over three years. He was about to experience the terror we now know as the Passion of the Christ. In His moment of prayer to God the Father, He said, *'Father, if it is Your will, take this cup away from Me; nevertheless, not My will, but Yours, be done.'* May we learn to pray like He prayed: *'Father Not my Will, but yours be done.'*

The third petition in the prayer the Lord taught us that we have all come to know as the Lord's prayer is *Your will be done.* As a friend of God, it is God's will that gets to be done in your life, not your will. It is not Stony's will anymore; it has got to be the Father's will always be done.

A friend of God prays daily: *'Your will be done.'* It is not your wife's will, your brother's, your father's, your mother's, or your sister's will. God's will ought to be what is done in your life. (Mark 8:34) says, Jesus, "*Whoever desires to come after Me, let him deny himself, and take up his cross, and follow Me.*" AW Tozer wrote "*The man with a cross no longer controls his destiny; he lost control when he picked up his cross. That cross immediately became to him an all-absorbing interest, an overwhelming interference. No matter what he may desire to do, there is but one thing he can do; that is, move on toward the place of crucifixion*".[3]

One of the early fathers and a man of God who was also the Patriarch of Antioch, Ignatius Theophorous said, "*Few souls understand what God would accomplish in them if they were to abandon themselves unreservedly to Him and if they were to allow His grace to mold them accordingly*".[4]

Do you want to be a friend of God? You've got to die to self. You've got to say, '*Enough of living for me, it is Christ now who lives in me. The life I now live is not my own, but it's the life of Christ lived by the faith of the Son of God in me.*'

In his book, Dangerous Calling, Paul David Tripp writes:

If you are ever going to be an ambassador in the hands of a God of glorious and powerful grace, you must die. You must die to your plans for your own life. You must die to your self-focused dreams of success. You must die to your demands for comfort and ease. You must die to your individual definition of the good life. You must die to your demands for pleasure, acclaim, prominence, and respect. You must die to your desire to be in control. You must die to your hope for independent righteousness. You must die to your plans for others. You must die to your cravings for a certain lifestyle or that particular location. You must die to your own kingship. You must die to the pursuit of your own glory in order to take up the cause of the glory of Another. You must die to your control over your own time. You must die to your maintenance of your own reputation. You must die to having the final answer and getting your own way. You must die to your unfaltering confidence in you. You must die.[5]

A true friend of God understands that everything they do in their lives ought to be done to the glory of God. As a friend of God, everything you do is for an audience of one – the Lord God almighty. You don't live your life to please others, whether they may be brother or sister or cousin; you live your life to please the almighty God. Paul puts it this way – *"Therefore, whether you eat or drink, or whatever you do, do all to the glory of God."* (1 Corinthians 10:31).

A true friend of God lays down their life for God all of the time. It may not involve you physically giving up the air you breathe, but it is certainly you not keeping anything to yourself. Do you want to be a friend of God, my friend? Well, it is time then to die to self and allow Christ to live in you. The life of a friend of God is a sold-out and laid-down life.

Chapter 12

Friendship With God Is Only Through Jesus Christ

*Jesus said to him, "I am the way, the truth, and the life. No one comes to the Father except through Me.- **(John 14:6)***

Friendship with God is only through Jesus Christ. After Adam's great and most consequential sin against God, a vast chasm was created, separating man from God. God, in His intrinsic nature, is holy and cannot co-exist with sin and iniquity. As a holy God, He couldn't mingle with the darkness that had corrupted humanity. For a really long time, most people could never draw near to Him. The Israelites, His chosen people, whom He had set apart for Himself, never lived up to the standard that He set out for them. Man's sins would constantly separate him from a holy God. The prophet Isaiah, being inspired by the Holy Spirit, said:

> *"Behold, the Lord's hand is not shortened,*
> *That it cannot save;*
> *Nor His ear heavy,*
> *That it cannot hear.*
> *But your iniquities have separated you from your*
> *God;*
> *And your sins have hidden His face from you,*
> *So that He will not hear.*
> *For your hands are defiled with [a]blood,*
> *And your fingers with iniquity;*

Friend Of God

Your lips have spoken lies,
Your tongue has muttered perversity."
(Isaiah 59:1-3).

Sin's power seemed to have overcome man as man became a slave to it. Humanity was without hope and vastly disconnected from God. The sacrifices prescribed for God's people were only temporary and could only go so far. Something so much better was direly needed. It had to be something permanent that would make it possible for any human with breath in their lungs to be reconciled with their Creator.

A permanent sacrifice had to be made. Not even any mere being could make this sacrifice. No angel in heaven or earth could accomplish this task of such colossal proportions. Only someone without sin or blemish Himself could make such a sacrifice. Only one who was fully God and fully man could accomplish this mission. That person, folks, was Jesus Christ, the ever-living Son of God. By dying on the cross of Calvary 2000 years ago, He made it possible for us all to become friends with the most high God as it had always been intended.

(Colossians 1:19 NLT) says, *'For God in all his fullness was pleased to live in Christ, and through Him God reconciled everything to Himself. He made peace with everything in heaven and on earth by means of Christ's blood on the cross'.*

When you read further, you will see that Paul says to all of us that we all *'were once alienated and enemies in your mind by wicked works, yet now He has reconciled in the body of his flesh through death to present you wholly and blameless and above reproach in his sight.'*

Friendship With God Is Only Through Jesus Christ

When Paul mentions *in His sight*, he is talking about in the sight of God.

It pleased God the Father that Jesus would be a bridge between God, the Father, and us, who are children of God. It pleased God the Father that by virtue of Jesus Christ, we become friends of our great God. God decreed that by virtue of the death of Jesus Christ, we who were once alienated from the commonwealth of salvation through God are now being adopted into the family of God. All of this, therefore, has become possible because of what Jesus Christ did on the cross.

Friends, I want to tell you that no one else can save you. No one else can create a path, a steadfast bridge to God for you, except Jesus Christ. I'm going to make it as clear as I can. No one else, no other person who has ever lived or who lives right now or who will live in the age to come, has ever or is ever going to be able to be a bridge between you and God the Father. No one else but the Lord Jesus Christ. No one else but the Messiah can be that bridge. No one else can be that bridge but the desire of Ages, Jesus Christ of Nazareth. Amen.

Let's read another scripture, shall we? (1 John 1:3) says, *'That which we have seen and heard we declare to you, that you also may have fellowship with us; and truly our fellowship is with the Father and with His Son Jesus Christ.'*

You could exchange the word fellowship for friendship as they speak of the same thing. Our friendship is with God the Father. Our fellowship is with God, the Father, and truly, our friendship is with the Father and His Son, Jesus Christ. How else can scripture make that clear to you if it's not been clear to you before? We have fellowship with God, the Father, and His Son, Jesus Christ. The Apostle John was saying, *'I've made this as clear as night and day to you. I have seen this. I have experienced this, and so now I declare this unto you that our fellowship is with God the Father and with Jesus Christ, His Son.'* That is indeed powerful, dear friend.

Jesus makes the same statement of Himself as the only path to friendship with God in another way. In (John 14:6), He declares, *'I am the way, the truth and the life. No one comes to the Father except through me.'* Jesus used the statement or the line "*I AM*" seven times. And of those seven declarations, this verse above contains the clearest picture of His role as mediator between God and man. If you have not believed the inspired words of Paul and Peter, well, right here, you have got the words of Jesus Himself.

Jesus is the only way to have a friendship with God. That is why I am so glad that He sought me and that He found me. I am so glad I am part of the Commonwealth of God's family. It is not because I was good enough, nor because I was smart enough, nor because I have abilities that others don't, nor because I can speak or write eloquently. No, no, no.

Nothing of that sort would have helped me stand scot-free and blameless before God. It's nothing but Jesus and Jesus alone. I want to repeat nothing, absolutely nothing, but Jesus and Jesus alone. Repeat those words in your heart, in your mind, and under the breath of your tongue. Nothing can save me but Jesus and Jesus alone, nothing can grant me peace but Jesus and Jesus alone, nothing else can give me pure and unbridled joy but Jesus and Jesus alone, and nothing can be a

Friendship With God Is Only Through Jesus Christ

bridge to God but Jesus alone. Nothing can create a path to friendship with God but Jesus and Jesus alone.

Now, there might be many who will offer an alternative path to God. Many others will offer you certain paths to spirituality, but I tell you, friend, they will only lead you to a fruitless end. Spirituality without Christ is worthless. You need Jesus and when you have got Jesus, He is all that you will ever need.

(Hebrews 1:1-5) declares *'God, who at various times and in various ways spoke in time past to the fathers by the prophets, has in these last days spoken to us by His Son, whom He has appointed heir of all things, through whom also He made the worlds; who being the brightness of His glory and the express image of His person, and upholding all things by the word of His power, when He had by Himself purged our sins, sat down at the right hand of the Majesty on high, having become so much better than the angels, as He has by inheritance obtained a more excellent name than they.'*

So, in past times, as we know in the Bible, God spoke through prophets like Isaiah, Jeremiah, Obadiah, Nahum, Samuel, Nathan, Elijah, and many others. God had spoken to the Commonwealth of Israel through these human oracles or messengers. In another chapter of this book, I wrote about how a friend of God speaks to God and hears from God. The only way we can maintain that friendship with God that enables us to speak to Him and hear from Him is through Jesus.

It is through Jesus alone, and I am grateful to God for Jesus. Thank you, Jesus, for being a bridge between me and the Father. It was a bridge I could not build on my own. It

Friend Of God

was a bridge I could not maintain on my own. I couldn't build it, and I certainly couldn't keep it intact. Only Jesus could, and only Jesus can, and only Jesus will ever be able to do so. So, friend, if you don't know Jesus and you desire to be a friend of God, realize that Jesus is your only hope and way to God.

If you say to yourself, 'I want to be a friend of the Creator of the universe; I want to be a friend of the One who holds the world in His hands,' I have got good news for you. I have got a cheat code, and it is very simple. Your path to friendship with God runs through Jesus Christ, the everlasting Son of God. It is not through the dead Buddha, the long-departed Confucius, or the deceased Muhammad. It is through the victorious risen Savior, Jesus Christ alone. It is through He who has conquered death once and for all, and His glorious name is Jesus Christ. His name is Yeshua Hamaschiach.

Let me pray for you today: *Lord, I thank you that our only path to God is through Jesus Christ of Nazareth. I am grateful that I could not build this bridge myself. I could not create this path or maintain it myself, but I'm glad that you did it for me. You paid the price for me. I was once alienated from God. We all were once alienated from the promise of God's friendship, but now we can hold on to friendship with God because of you, Jesus. Thank you, Jesus. Thank you, Heavenly Father. Thank you, God, for becoming a faithful and true friend of mine. Blessed be your holy name. In Jesus' name, we pray. Amen.*

Chapter 13

God's Friends Love Others

If someone says, "I love God," and hates his brother, he is a liar; for he who does not love his brother whom he has seen, how can he love God whom he has not seen?
(1 John 4:20)

A friend of God loves the Lord and because they love the Lord, they're able to love others because when a man is full of the love of God, they overflow in love for others. It's like the Psalm that says, *You make my cup to overflow.*

When God fills you up with so much of His love, His unending love, His great and colossal love; what ends up happening is that out of that wellspring of love that you found yourself in, you are able to love others. You can't love others as you need to love them if you yourself are not bathing in the love of God. However, when you are bathing in the love of God and when you are rooted and deeply grounded in the love of God, it is so easy to love others because you see how God has loved you, and then you can't help but love your brothers in the same way God has loved you. When you look at your life and see how God loves you; you can't help but love others. Here are some ways that friends of God display the Love of Christ:

- When we forgive others even when they don't deserve it.

- When we try to meet their present need and not ignore it.

- When we season our speech with grace even when the recipients don't deserve it.

- When we reach out to others with the message of the gospel.

- When we don't kick others when they are down but seek to have them lifted up and restored.

- When we tell a broken world that they need Jesus as the solution to the ills that plague them.

- When we take care of the unfortunate, needy, oppressed, persecuted, and disadvantaged.

- When we care for those in the household of the faith (Christ's Body – His Church).

The church in Korea blossomed mightily because Christians took the pain to care for poverty and war-stricken Koreans in the aftermath of the Korean War. The church, throughout the bubonic plagues of the Medieval Age, stood out for the love and compassion that was on display when everyone else was focused on their own well-being in selfishness.

Never forget that the reason that you will be able to do all of the above is His love for you. It is out of that vertical love that you are able to love your fellow man as God desires you to do. We love others because He first loved us. The great expositor, Alexander MacLaren urges us to *"remember where the sweet reciprocation and interchange of love begins. We have to turn to that heavenly Friend, and feel that as life itself, so the love which is the life of life, has its beginning in Him, and that never would our hearts have turned themselves from their alienation, unless there had poured down upon them the attractive outflow of His great love"*.

The love of Christ compels me to love others. The love of Christ changes me into such a new man that I can't help but love other people. God's love is not selfish, so you end up wanting others to experience what you are experiencing. In that manner, therefore, preaching the gospel to others is not just an obligation or tedious responsibility. You just get to do it because you are so full of God's love. You just get to love others because you are so full of God's love. You don't do it just because God wants you to do it. Yes, doing something because God commands you is important, but your duty of love comes first. You tell others about the Lord because you love them and because Christ has first loved you.

This is what Paul meant when he said, *"For the love of Christ compels us, because we judge thus: that if One died for all, then all died; and He died for all, that those who live should live no longer for themselves, but for Him who died for them and rose again."* (2 Corinthians 5:14).

Because of how much of God's love I am full of, I can't just help but love others with His love. (Romans 8:28) says, "We *know that all things work together for the good of them who love God and are called according to His purpose.*" There are so many benefits to being a friend of God, because all things begin to work together for your good. But most importantly, you love the Lord, and you love others because you are deeply

Friend Of God

grounded and rooted in the love of God. That's what friendship with God will do.

Friendship with God will cause you to be so full of His love that you can't help but love Him and love others, amen. The love of Christ changes us, folks. The love of Christ touches the very embers of our hearts and transforms us, and we are never the same again. God's friends love God, and they love others, not because they are told to, even though that's part of it, but because they're overwhelmed with the love of God themselves, and they can't help but love God and love others.

Chapter 14

God's Friends Obey God

"You are My friends if you do whatever I command you."
- (John 15:14).

The book of John is one of my favorite books in the whole Bible. It has a certain uniqueness to it that makes it stand apart from the other synoptic gospels.

The Gospel of Matthew focuses on Jesus as the Messiah, bringing the kingdom of Heaven to us. It is targeted at a Jewish audience. The Book of Mark, being the shortest of the synoptic gospels, focuses more on the acts of Jesus than His words. The gospel of Luke is very much written in a prose-like pattern. It is a collection of stories about the Lord and is very detailed.

The Gospel of John, however, centers its focus on the words of our Lord Jesus Himself and His divinity. The words of our Savior, as written in that book, always create a chill all through my body whenever I listen to or read it. In it, I constantly hear the words of our dear Lord pierce through my heart. In the book of John, our Lord goes the distance in teaching us about the intimate friendship and connection He wants to have with us, who are His bride. In (John 14, 15), this is made very apparent.

If you have studied the words of Jesus for any decent amount of time, you would realize that there are certain statements He makes with added emphasis or repetitively. That is not a random decision on His part. When the Lord repeats His emphasis on a point, it is because He wants to truly sink it into your spirit man.

All through the gospels, He uses statements like *Verily, verily I say unto you,* T*ruly truly I say*, or *Assuredly*. In the 14th and 15th chapters of John, however, He resorts more to just repeating the same statement over and over again with greater elaboration each time.

In (John 14:15), He says, *"If you love me, keep my commands."* In verse 21, again, He says, '*Whoever has my commands and keeps them is the one who loves me. The one who loves me will be loved by my Father, and I too will love them and show myself to them.*' In verses 23-24, again, He says, '*Anyone who loves me will obey my teaching. My Father will love them, and we will come to them and make our home with them. Anyone who does not love me will not obey my teaching. These words you hear are not my own; they belong to the Father who sent me.*' In (John 15:10), He says again, '*If you keep my commands, you will remain in my love, just as I have kept my Father's commands and remain in his love.*'

These repetitions are so important to understanding the heart of our Lord. He was trying to hammer home the idea that if you love Him, then you ought to keep His commands, and so if you don't love Him, then you won't bother about keeping His commandments. He who receives and keeps the commands of the Lord is He who loves the Lord. That, of course, means that he or she who does not keep His commandments does not love Him.

God's Friends Obey God

It is very easy to say I love Jesus. You have probably heard that statement a lot. What you don't see often is people following up on the actions that indicate that they love the Lord. I will refer briefly to the popular maxim that says, '*It is easier said than done.*'

Every friendship that exists has rules. There are certain things you do in order to be called a friend of someone else. The rule for being a friend of the Lord is that you are obedient to His words to you. His rules are that you follow His commands. You follow what He has to say because if you do not do that, well, you're not a friend of God. This is not some theologian or some flimsy preacher telling you this. These are the words of Jesus that you have read.

Jerry Bridges said, "*The daily experience of Christ's love is linked to our obedience to Him. It is not that His love is conditioned on our obedience. That would be legalism. But our experience of His love is dependent upon our obedience*".[1]

If you see someone who says they're a Christian, but they do not follow any commands of the Lord Jesus, well, they're not friends of Jesus, and they're not friends of God. They do not love Him. They do not love Jesus, the Son of God who was sent to die for their sins.

The utmost sign that you can call yourself a friend of God or one who loves God is that you follow what Jesus had to say and what the Lord Himself has commanded in His word. Do you love the Lord? Do you follow His commands? It's as simple as ABC. Your obedience to the Lord is the only way to deepen your fellowship with Him. Oswald Chambers, the author of My Utmost of His Highest, said, "*If I obey Jesus Christ in the seemingly random circumstances of life, they become pinholes through which I see the face of God."*[2]

Let us read the Gospel of (Matthew 12:46-50):

46 *"While Jesus was still talking to the crowd, his mother and brothers stood outside, wanting to speak to him.*

47 *Someone told him, "Your mother and brothers are standing outside, wanting to speak to you."*

48 *He replied to him, "Who is my mother, and who are my brothers?"*

49 *Pointing to his disciples, he said, "Here are my mother and my brothers.*

50 *For whoever does the will of my Father in heaven is my brother and sister and mother."*

Now, in this scripture, it wasn't like Jesus was trying to disown His earthly parents while He was on this earth. What He was trying to do was place a heavy emphasis on following the commands of God and how that is crucial in a relationship with God. He was trying to tell us something really important to the heart of God. What, then, was that message He was trying to send across? It was that *He who does the will of my Father in heaven, that is my brother, that is my sister, that is my mother, that is my daughter. He who does the will of God, he who bends himself or herself to the will of God, he or she who devotes themselves to following the commands from God, that is who I can say is a friend of God.*

I will bring to remembrance a verse that you saw at the start of this chapter that basically encapsulates this. (John

God's Friends Obey God

15:14) says, *"You are My friends if you do whatever I command you."* A friend of God obeys the words of God.

King David, in (Psalms 24), writes:

> *3 "Who may ascend into the hill of the Lord?*
> *Or who may stand in His holy place?*
> *4 He who has clean hands and a pure heart,*
> *Who has not lifted up his soul to an idol,*
> *Nor sworn deceitfully.*
> *5 He shall receive blessing from the Lord,*
> *And righteousness from the God of his salvation.*
> *6 This is Jacob, the generation of those who seek Him,*
> *Who seek Your face." Selah*

This is a famous portion of scripture that has been turned into so many songs. However, I want you to focus on verses 3 and 4 for a second. He starts verse 3 with a question, which is *Who may ascend into the hill of the Lord, Or who may stand in His holy place?* He was *asking who may get into God's presence, who will get to call themselves friends of God, who will stand in this holy place to communicate with God, to have a chitchat with God, to have a heart-to-heart discussion with God to have a prayer session and a fellowship with God?*

The man or woman who gets to do so is he or she who has clean hands and a pure heart. It is he or she who has not lifted up their soul to an idol. It is he or she who follows God's commands. It is he or she who obeys God. Oh friend, obedience to God is necessary; it is absolutely necessary. It's paramount to being called a friend of God. If you want to be a friend of God, you've got to know how to obey God, for a true friend of God obeys God.

The 14th-century English preacher, Robert Cawdrey said, *"If thou wilt bend thyself to obedience, and to a virtuous and godly life, thou shalt ever have him a strong rock, whereupon thou mayst boldly build a castle and tower of defense. He will be unto thee a mighty pillar, bearing up heaven and earth, where to thou mayst lean and not be deceived, wherein thou mayst trust and not be disappointed."*[3]

Obedience, my friends, is an act of worship. God rewards those who obey Him with His presence. My favorite worship leader of all time, Darlene Zscech, said, '*Every time you open up your heart in obedience to God and worship Him with all your heart, all your mind, and all your soul, our beautiful Lord responds with His magnificent presence.*'[4]

It is an act of worship that's much more preferable to any other act of sacrifice. In response to King Saul not obeying the word of the Lord to Saul through the Prophet Samuel, Samuel declared:

> *"Does the Lord delight in burnt offerings*
> *and sacrifices as much as in obeying the Lord?*
> *To obey is better than sacrifice,*
> *and to heed is better than the fat of rams."*
> **(1 Samuel 15:22-23 MEV).**

God values an obedient child of His and considers an obedient child His friend. Moses was a friend of God who generally obeyed God throughout his life, but one instance of disobedience to God caused him to miss out on entering the Promise Land:

God's Friends Obey God

"Then Moses lifted his hand and hit the rock twice with his stick [staff; he was supposed to speak to it. Water began pouring out, and the people [community, congregation, assembly] and their animals drank it.

But the Lord said to Moses and Aaron, "Because you did not believe [trust] me, and because you did not honor me as holy [show my holiness] before the people [L sons/T children of Israel], you will not lead them [L this community; congregation; assembly] into the land I will give them." **(Numbers 20:11-12, Expanded Bible).**

When you look at the people who obeyed God in scripture, you can clearly tell they were close friends of God. Abraham, who God called His friend, obeyed God when the Lord told him to leave the land of Ur and go to a place that He would show Him. He also obeyed and believed God when God told Him He would have a son at a very old age. He obeyed God when God told him to take Isaac, his precious son, and sacrifice him on the top of the mountain. Abraham was very obedient to God's instructions, and God called him a friend because of his obedient heart.

Noah obeyed God when He was told to build an ark even when the world had never seen rain like that of the flood.

David always obeyed the instructions of the Lord whenever He inquired and prayed about decisions to take. In (Psalm 119:11), David said, *'Your word I have hidden in my heart, that I might not sin against You.'*

Joseph always obeyed God and walked with integrity even when temptations arose that would have caused him to do the opposite.

Friend Of God

Joshua always obeyed whatever the Lord told him to do as he fought many of Israel's enemies.

Esther obeyed God and made a case for her people even though it came at great risk to her.

The Prophet Samuel always obeyed God, and every word God spoke through Him came to pass.

Mary obeyed and believed God when she got word that she would carry the Savior of the human race in her womb.

One beautiful thing about obeying God is that you don't get to do it in your ability. God is not up there in heaven saying *you have to do your best to follow me using all of your might.*

He helps us obey His commands through His Holy Spirit. His power within us enables us to attend to every obligation that He has tasked us with.

I am so thankful that in the Holy Spirit, I have a helper who will aid me in doing God's will and pleasing the Father. St Augustine prayed, *"Give me the grace [O Lord] to do as You command, and command me to do what You will! ... O holy God...when Your commands are obeyed, it is from You that we receive the power to obey them."*[5]

I am so glad that I didn't get to live out the Christian life in my own strength and ability. I have got the Spirit of the Living God to help me. The Greek appellation Jesus used to describe the Holy Spirit is the word *'Paraclete.'* It translates as "advocate," "intercessor," "teacher," "helper," and "comforter."

God's Friends Obey God

The Holy Spirit is all of those things to every child of God, and He will empower us to fulfill the desires of our great God. He will help us perform all that the Lord tasks us with. He will help us obey God in everything and, in so doing, touch God's heart and bring a smile to His face. Look up to the Lord and say, '*Holy Spirit help me obey and fulfill God's will for my life and help me please God.*' I assure you: He will do just that.

Chapter 15

God's Friends Are Passionate About God's Kingdom And The Gospel

My love for your house burns in me like a fire, and when others insult you, they insulted me as well.
– *(Psalm 69:9 NLT)*

The heart of a friend of God is moved by what moves God's heart. A friend of God is broken by the same things that break the heart of God. So, ask yourself, what does God hate? And ask yourself, do I hate those things too? What and who does God love? Do I love them and those things, too? Ask yourself if you are in God's calendar and agenda or if you are in the way of it. God can give you His passions and desires, and He wants to. Of all the passions that the Lord has given to me, preaching the gospel of Jesus Christ and caring for the persecuted Church stand out.

Scripture declares, "*The Lord is not slack concerning His promise, as some count slackness, but is longsuffering toward us, not willing that any should perish but that all should come to repentance.*" (2 Peter 3:9).

The salvation of souls, therefore, is a big deal to the Lord. All of Heaven celebrates in joy when one sinner turns to the Lord (Luke 15:10).

God's Friends Are Passionate About God's Kingdom And The Gospel

You may have a different burden than what the Lord has given to me. It might be caring for victims of human trafficking. It might be caring for the poor and the oppressed. It might be caring for the addicts, the abused, and the broken in society. It might be caring for the disabled or less privileged. Whatever it might be, a friend of God is passionate about what God is passionate about. Whatever breaks God's heart ought to break yours, too.

The great Charles Spurgeon said, "*We are mirrors reflecting the transactions of Calvary, telescopes manifesting the distant glories of an exalted Redeemer*".[1] As friends of God, we ought to reflect the heart of God.

A great Scottish Baptist preacher wrote beautifully about God's friends taking up God's interests:

"If we are God's 'friends and lovers He will take up our cause. Be sure that if God be for us, it matters not who is against us. If we are God's friends and lovers we have to take up His cause. What would you think of a man who, in going away to a far-off country, said to some friend, 'I wish you would look after so and so for me as long as I am gone'; and the friend would say 'Yes!' and never give a thought nor lift a finger to discharge the obligation? God trusts His reputation to you Christian people; He has interests in this world that you have to look after. You have to defend Him as really as He has to defend you. And it is the dreadful contradiction of religious people's profession of religion that they often care so little, and do so little to promote the cause, to defend the name, to adorn the reputation, and to further what I may venture to call the interests, of their heavenly Friend in the world".[2]

We can't take on all of the tasks God wants accomplished on the earth, and I am glad we don't get to do that. After all, He is God, and we are not. He is always dealing with multiple

Friend Of God

things at the same time, and we can hardly focus on accomplishing one thing sometimes. But I am glad that He gets to allow us to be partners in what He wants to do across the earth. You become a friend of God when God's desires become your desires. Amen.

In this chapter, I am choosing to put the spotlight on various ministries that I strongly believe are involved in work that is very dear to the heart of God. The nature of their ministries is very diverse, but they are all united in their work for the proclamation of the gospel and the welfare of fellow brothers and sisters in Christ. I have divided these ministries into two groups. The first group of ministries are evangelistic in nature and are consumed with the desire to take the gospel of Christ to every corner of the globe, from America to the ends of the earth.

The second group is ministries that are focused on the welfare of persecuted Christians around the world. These ministries help aid the millions of Christians who are being persecuted simply because they believe in our Lord Jesus as we all do and long to share His gospel of peace and freedom with their neighbors.

Did you know that about 365 million Christians around the world live under some form of persecution simply for their faith in Jesus Christ? That is 25 million more people than the population of the United States, which is the 3rd largest country in the world by population. That is 15% of the 2.4 billion people on earth who profess faith in Christ around the earth. That is a lot of people who suffer for their faith in our Savior.

God's Friends Are Passionate About God's Kingdom And The Gospel

I believe with all of my heart that the plight of persecuted Christians is very close to the heart of God. I am so glad, however, that Scripture tells us that *the Lord is close to the brokenhearted and saves those who are crushed in spirit* (Psalm 34:18, NIV). These words from the Apostle Paul prick my heart daily: *Therefore, as we have opportunity, let us do good to all, especially to those who are of the household of faith.* (Galatians 6:10). Friend, I implore in the name of Christ whom you love and adore that you do all you can to support the plight of persecuted Christians.

These two groups of ministries (evangelistic and welfare for persecuted Christians) represent the core passions God has placed in my heart. For me, these are issues that are very close to the heart of the Lord, and He has truly burdened my heart with the causes of preaching the gospel of His kingdom, which is Good News, and the welfare of persecuted Christians who don't enjoy the freedoms that we enjoy in America and the wider western world.

These two causes are reflected in the vision and mission of a ministry I lead: *Stony Kalango Ministries*. It is an evangelistic ministry that exists for the purpose of spreading the fame of Jesus across America and around the world. We are purposefully intentional about seeing the name of Jesus lifted high all around the globe as the scriptures prophesy in (Habakkuk 2:15) which says '*For the earth will be filled with the knowledge of the glory of the Lord, as the waters cover the sea*'. It is our desire that many come to know God in such a radically transforming manner, and that through that, our culture is shaped for God's glory, for truly our God reigns. On the other hand, we are passionate about the plight of persecuted Christians around the world and seek to play a part in supporting them as needed. Our ultimate desire is to see the Lord glorified through the ministry that He has entrusted us with. You can find out more about us on our website – **stonykalango.com**.

There are also other ministries that are likeminded and I also wanted to put the spotlight on them. These ministries range from denominational to non-denominational and independent ministries but are all focused on the vision the Almighty God has given them. These ministries are organizations that I believe walk in integrity and are truly passionate about their missions and vision. These ministries have all largely shown proper Christian financial stewardship, and I hope you can join me in supporting any one of your choices, depending on what the Lord draws your heart towards. Their inclusion in this list indicates my recommendation of them as long as they continue to hold to the orthodoxy of the faith and the integrity that comes with a God-centered ministry.

List of Evangelism Ministries

Christ for All Nations: CFAN, as they are sometimes called, is an amazing evangelistic ministry that has seen some of the greatest harvest of souls for the Kingdom of God I have ever seen. This ministry was founded and led for decades by Evangelist Reinhardt Bonnke, who held large open-air gospel crusades that saw hundreds of thousands of people hear the gospel in single nightly meetings. CFAN has been majorly focused for decades on preaching the gospel in Africa, and Evangelist Reinhardt Bonnke saw about 79 million recorded decisions for Christ in his long decades of ministry.

God's Friends Are Passionate About God's Kingdom And The Gospel

Daniel Kolenda succeeded Evangelist Bonnke and has continued his legacy of holding large gospel crusades to reach the lost and draw them to Christ. I personally attended one of Evangelist Reinhardt Bonnke's crusade meetings as a young kid, where I witnessed countless hundreds of thousands of people hearing the gospel. I love this ministry, and it is one that Olivia and I personally support in a financial capacity. Oh, how we need millions to hear the gospel preached again and again. The website for Christ For All Nations is www.cfan.org

Sat 7: When you think about the Arab world, the notion of Islam or Muslim nations probably comes to mind before anything else. In most countries in the Middle East, the Gospel cannot be freely preached as we can preach here in the West. A lot of Christians who suffer persecution do so because they live in Muslim-majority countries. Sat 7 is an amazing media ministry that is focused on reaching the regions of North Africa and the Middle East, most of which is the Arab World. What an amazing ministry this is, and it is so needed for such a time as this. I truly thank God for the work that they are able to do. Praise Jesus! Their website address is www.sat7usa.org

One for Israel: This is an amazing evangelical ministry focused on reaching Jews, mostly those who live in Israel. They exercise such a patient, thoughtful, and loving approach to communicating the gospel, and I have enjoyed watching their video content on YouTube. It brings joy to my heart to see how they are taking the message of Christ once again to skeptical Jews and allowing them to hear the same good news that was preached by the Messiah to Jews 2000 years ago. Their website address is www.oneforisrael.org

Friend Of God

Gideons International: Everyone who has stayed at hotels long enough has probably seen a Gideons Bible in their hotel room. This ministry that shares free Bibles all across the world has had an impact that they will only fully understand in Heaven. I believe the world has been blessed by this ministry, and its efforts have been monumental for the kingdom of God. Their website address is www.gideons.org

Assemblies of God World Missions: This ministry is the major missionary arm of the Assemblies of God USA in relation to missions and evangelization. They support about 2,900 missionaries and associates around the globe. Their mission is to establish the Church among all peoples everywhere by reaching, planting, training, and serving. The Assemblies of God World Missions is one of the largest denominational mission organizations that sends out the most missionaries to the world. Their website is www.agwm.org

Wycliffe Bible Translators USA: This ministry was founded by William Cameron Townsend in 1946 and named after John Wycliffe, the first man to fully translate the Bible into English. The impact of this ministry in the kingdom of God has just been simply colossal. They have had the Bible translated into over 700 languages since they began and are today one of the largest Bible translation organizations in the world. With a dream to have the Bible translated into every known and spoken language on earth, they have answered Christ's call to carry the gospel to the ends of the earth. What an amazing ministry they are. I truly praise the Lord for the impact they have had over decades of ministry. Their website is www.wycliffe.org

God's Friends Are Passionate About God's Kingdom And The Gospel

International Missions Board: This ministry is the major missionary arm of the Southern Baptist Convention. They state that they seek to take the gospel to every nation, all tribes, peoples, and languages. Today, the IMB supports over 3,500 field missionaries and personnel and 123 global missionary partners. They are the largest missionary organization in the United States and do great work in reaching unreached people with the gospel of Christ. Their vision is to see a multitude from every nation, tribe, people, and language, who worship the Lord Jesus Christ. Their website is www.imb.org

Billy Graham Evangelistic Association: Just about every Christian in the United States knows the name Billy Graham. Even though he has gone to be with the Lord in heaven, his impact is still very much alive today. His evangelistic ministry, the Billy Graham Evangelistic Association, still does an amazing job of taking the gospel to everyone they can. Franklin Graham has continued that legacy doing a lot of humanitarian work alongside the gospel ministry. Their website is www.billygraham.org

Chris Mikkelson Ministries: This ministry is very similar to Christ For All Nations which I have written about earlier. In fact, Evangelist Mikkelson was trained as an evangelist through CFAN. According to the Ministry website, Chris Mikkelson Ministries *'was birthed in 2015 with the sole purpose of fulfilling the Great Commission. We accomplish this through our mass Gospel crusades, church and revival services, television programming, podcasts, and social media platforms. Our international crusades are strategically planned in the most unreached parts of the world where Christianity is only 2% or less. We work with local churches in the region to disciple the new believers and oftentimes, many new churches* *are planted from each crusade.*' This ministry has largely been focused on reaching the nation of Pakistan, which is a Muslim-majority nation where Christians face persecution for their faith. Their website is www.chrismikkelson.com

Andres Bisonni Ministries: This is another amazing ministry that takes the gospel of Christ to the lost. Andres Bisonni emphasizes his dependence on the aid of the Holy Spirit in preaching the Good News. Their evangelistic meetings have mostly been held in Central and South American countries, and a multitude of people have come to know the Lord through this ministry. The ministry's website is www.holyspirit.tv

Brad Hofen Ministries: You may have never heard of Brad Hofen Ministries, but it is mentioned here because I personally know and have been to many church services with this great man of God. I have quietly followed his ministry, keeping up with the letters his ministry regularly sends out to its friends and partners. They do amazing work for the gospel of Christ in India, a nation that is increasingly becoming more hostile to carriers of the gospel due to a spike in Hindu nationalist movements that see the growth of Christianity as a threat to their centuries-old religion. Please pray for this precious ministry and support them in whatever capacity you can, whether through word or deed.

Shake the Nations with Nathan Morris: According to their website, Evangelist Nathan, his wife, Rachel, and the STN team travel around the world with a passion to preach the Gospel to all nations and to see the power of the Holy Spirit demonstrated through signs, wonders, and miracles. To date, they have seen countless decisions for Christ, with many

God's Friends Are Passionate About God's Kingdom And The Gospel

more reached through worldwide media. The ministry is also involved in humanitarian outreaches that serve the poor and needy with the love of Jesus Christ. The ministry's website address is www.shakethenations.com

Every Home for Christ: This ministry states that their purpose is to carry Christ to everyone, everywhere, in every generation, and to inspire and empower the Church to carry Christ to their world. They provide training and kingdom resources that help equip churches and ministers of the gospel in their indigenous local contexts. Between 2019 and 2023, they have made over 868 million gospel presentations, whether through mail, media, events, or digital propagation of the gospel. I would say that they did amazing work for such a short duration. Their website address is www.everyhome.org

Youth for Christ: With over 116 chapters across the U.S. and U.S. military bases, YFC reaches young people everywhere, working together with the local Church and other like-minded partners to raise up lifelong followers of Jesus who lead by their godliness in lifestyle, devotion to the Word of God and prayer, passion for sharing the love of Christ, and commitment to social involvement. Their website address is www.YFC.net

Village Missions: Village Missions state that they are committed to helping country churches not only survive but thrive. They say: since 1948, we have been helping country churches thrive all across North America. We place pastors in rural churches and help those churches get back on their feet. We care about the country church and are working to keep the Church a vibrant and vital presence in more than 230 rural communities throughout North America. We were here when the crisis hit, and the community was searching for somewhere to turn for answers. If your heart is geared towards the work of the Lord in Rural America, you might consider being of assistance to this wonderful ministry. Their website address is www.villagemissions.org

Other Worthy Mentions, Their Vision and Mission

Commission to Every Nation

What they do (*In their own words*): CTEN is a servant organization that helps missionaries fulfill the unique vision God has given them. Through administrative support, we provide accountability and help the missionary get to the field. Through pastoral care, we help them remain effective and healthy while they are there. Their website address is www.cten.org

Mission Aviation Fellowship:

What they do (*In their own words*): Each year, MAF provides aviation services to more than 400 mission agencies, churches, and humanitarian organizations around the world. Without MAF, some of these organizations would be unable to reach the people they serve. Through these partnerships, MAF connects isolated people with vital services and goods while tangibly sharing the love of Christ.

Mission Aviation Fellowship's Vision and Mission: To see isolated people changed by the love of Christ, serving together to bring help, hope, and healing through aviation. Their website address is www.maf.org

God's Friends Are Passionate About God's Kingdom And The Gospel

Send International

Who they are and what they do: *Send International* partners with churches to send missionaries from many nations to the unreached in Asia, Eurasia, and North America.

Mission: To mobilize God's people and engage the unreached in order to establish reproducing churches. Their website address is www.send.org

Youth With A Mission:

Who they are and what they do (*In their own words*): Youth With A Mission is a global movement of Christians from many cultures, age groups, and Christian traditions dedicated to serving Jesus throughout the world. Also known as YWAM (pronounced "WHY-wham"), we unite in a common purpose to know God and to make Him known. Back when we began in 1960, our main focus was to help youth get involved in missions. Today, we still focus on youth and include people of all ages. We currently have tens of thousands of staff (called "YWAMers") from nearly every country, including places like Indonesia, Nepal, Mozambique, and Colombia. Their vision and mission is to know God and to make Him known. Their website address is www.ywam.org

Hutchcraft Ministries

Who they are and what they do (*In their own words*): Today, Hutchcraft Ministries remains all about "Communicating Christ to the Lost in their Language," and their ministry team is passionate about sharing the Good News of Jesus with today's generation. They seek to reach lost people where they are, and in ways, they will understand.

Friend Of God

Vision and Mission (*In their own words*): Hutchcraft Ministries is all about "spiritual rescue." The mission statement of Jesus is "to seek and to save the lost" (Luke 19:10). Hutchcraft Ministries seeks to join Jesus in this mission by sharing the unchanging Gospel message of Jesus with a world of lost people. The ministry team of creative writers and producers makes art that will change lives. Through short films, printed material, websites, and social media, Hutchcraft Ministries seeks to address felt needs that will lead people to the cross of Jesus Christ. Their website address is www.hutchcraft.com

International Students: This is a ministry that rings close to home and one I have an affinity for. I was once an international student here in the United States. Even though I am fully baked into the American system today, I was once that little Nigerian kid on foreign shores who the Lord had helped fulfill a long-held and cherished dream. They say: with the millions of international students on American, Canadian, and British shores coming from every corner of the earth, we have such a wealth of opportunities to take the gospel even while in our local communities. It used to be that we would always have to go to the end of the world to reach the lost and praise God for that, but friend, the world is now coming to us, and my question for you is – What are you doing about that? This ministry is one of the few with a vision and mission centered on the many international shores that come to American shores. Praise God for them. Their website address is www.internationalstudents.org

Haggai International

Vision and Mission (*In their own words*): Our vision is to see every nation redeemed and transformed through the Gospel of Jesus Christ. There is no shortcut, no easy way. Governments cannot bring peace. Education cannot bring salvation. Business and industry cannot bring healing. Psychology and sociology cannot bring joy. Only Jesus can bring reconciliation to the world.

Who They Are and What They Do (*In their own words*): We select, equip, multiply, and encourage difference-makers all across the globe. We have equipped and believe that strategically positioned, influential leaders are catalysts for local people experiencing life change, community transformation, and nations being redeemed. We also believe leaders need equipping and encouragement to achieve exponential impact and sustainable momentum. We have over 135,000 strategically positioned leaders in 189 nations who are committed to ending Gospel poverty.

Our leaders have a distinct advantage. We are called to inspire and equip those already living, working, and serving in the places where Gospel poverty exists. We believe our leaders possess a clear advantage in reaching their own people with the Gospel. Their website address is www.haggai-international.org

List of Care and Relief Ministries for the Persecuted Church.

Open Doors: Open Doors was founded by Andrew van der Bijl, or Brother Andrew, as he was fondly called. He was known for smuggling Bibles into Poland, which was under the tyranny of communism at the time. He also engaged in smuggling Bibles to a lot of Soviet-led Eastern European countries and put his life in danger for the cause of Christ. The ministry grew in size and scale and even embarked on a successful mission of smuggling a million Bibles into China using a semi-submersible that evaded Chinese military ships. This is an amazing ministry that has done so much for the kingdom of God, especially those of the household of the faith. Their website address is www.opendoors.org

The Voice of the Martyrs: VOM, as they are called, is another amazing ministry that *'serves persecuted Christians in the world's most difficult and dangerous places to follow Christ.'* Founded by Richard and Sabina Wurmbrand in 1967, VOM started after Richard was imprisoned for preaching Christ in Communist Romania. *'Since 1967, VOM has been dedicated to inspiring all believers to a biblical faith by telling the stories of persecuted Christians, thereby inspiring a deeper commitment to Christ and the fulfillment of his Great Commission, no matter the cost.'* I have received and obtained several books and resources from this amazing ministry, and I can assure you they are constantly out there in the frontline trenches fighting for our fellow persecuted believers in Christ. Richard Wurmbrand blazed the trail for a lot of ministries that assist persecuted and afflicted Christians and is indeed a giant of the faith. I am sure, though I never met him personally, that he was a friend of God. Their website address is www.persecution.com

Global Christian Relief – This is an offshoot arm of the International Open Doors Ministry. They were formerly called Open Doors USA and basically carried out the same ministry of caring for the persecuted Church as Open Doors does. Their website address is www.globalchristianrelief.org

Release International: Release International describes their ministry as a *UK-based Christian ministry, supporting believers around the world who are persecuted for Christ and the gospel.* They were inspired by the life and witness of Pastor Richard Wurmbrand, who spent 14 years in communist prisons. Pastor Richard himself started Voice of the Martyrs, a ministry I discussed earlier. They assert that they are driven by the command in Hebrews, which says, *'Continue to remember those in prison as if you were together with them in prison, and those who are mistreated, as if you yourselves were suffering.'* (Hebrews 13:3; NIV; 2011). They are currently active in around 30 countries where they prayerfully, pastorally, and practically do all they can to love and serve persecuted Christians. Their website is www.releaseinternational.org

Help the Persecuted: This ministry serves mainly in Muslim nations that are hostile to the gospel of Christ and where persecution of Christians for their faith is all too common. They describe themselves as ministers of the Gospel whose mission is to *rescue persecuted believers escaping imminent danger. They believe they also have to restore them to full physical, emotional, and spiritual health. Help the Persecuted believes they also ought to help rebuild their lives, empowering them to thrive as disciples of Christ in hostile places.* Their website is www.htp.org

International Christian Concern (*In their own words*): Since ICC's creation in 1995, we have developed an effective and efficient system of bringing relief to persecuted Christians in need. We team up with trustworthy partners on the ground to develop and implement both immediate aid and long-term assistance projects. We then monitor our projects to ensure faithfulness to biblical principles and wise stewardship of funds. Persecution is a multifaceted problem that requires a comprehensive solution. For nearly three decades, ICC has developed a unique approach focused on Assistance, Advocacy, and Awareness. We exist to bandage the wounds of persecuted Christians and to build the Church in the most challenging parts of the world. Their website address is www.persecution.org

Christian Solidarity Worldwide (*In their own words*)

Mission and Vision

Our vision is to have a world free from religious persecution, where everyone can practice a religion or belief of their choice.

As a Christian organization standing up for religious freedom, our mission is to:

- Stand with those facing injustice because of their religious beliefs.

- Communicate a Christian rationale of religious freedom for all.

- Raise public consciousness of religious persecution, building a movement committed to prayer and action.

- Encourage the U.S. government to aggressively and effectively pursue its policy of promoting religious freedom worldwide. Their website is www.cswusa.org

Christian Freedom International (*In their own words*)

Who They Are and What They Do: We are a non-denominational human rights organization providing real solutions to conditions of oppression and misery caused by religious persecution. Christian Freedom International (CFI) aids, equips, and advocates for Christians who are oppressed or persecuted for their faith. Since 1998, Christian Freedom International has worked alongside persecuted Christians to provide aid in high-risk countries. We help with emergency relief, safe houses, Bibles, discipleship training, and more. Located next to Washington, DC, we advocate for Christians who suffer for their faith to key government officials.

Mission and Vision

CFI provides spiritual and physical help for suffering Christians to live in the dignity of God's love and rise above their circumstances.

CFI offers ways for Christians to ease the burdens of persecuted Christians through prayer, action, and giving. Their website is www.christianfreedom.org

China Aid (*In their own words*): China Aid assists persecuted people groups and rights activists located in China. We accomplish these goals via our 3 Es: exposing the abuses, encouraging the abused, and equipping leaders of persecuted groups.

China Aid exposes the oppression by writing news stories on them in both English and Chinese. We also have an advocacy initiative in which we testify in front of prominent policymakers and government bodies, including the U.S.

Congress and the United Nations. Often, persecution also puts families under duress.

In order to encourage the abused, we developed our Family of Prisoners fund, which provides for their various needs. One example of this is the Lin Zhao Freedom Award, which grants a cash prize to people who have made great sacrifices for their promotion of freedom and democracy.

China Aid also equips people undergoing persecution by providing theological and legal training for them. This gives them the spiritual fortitude to withstand oppression while facing their legal battles with knowledge of their full rights according to both Chinese and international law. Their website is www.chinaaid.org

Persecution Project Foundation (*In their own words*): Persecution Project is a non-denominational faith-based organization providing active compassion for the persecuted with special emphasis on the war-torn nation of Sudan. We bring crisis relief and spiritual hope to victims of civil war, genocide, and religious persecution. We also provide on-the-ground assistance while restoring hope and rebuilding communities through the love of Christ Jesus.

Persecution Project was founded in 1997 by Brad Phillips. In 1998, Brad traveled to war-ravaged Sudan and shot hours of video chronicling brutal persecution against Christians by the Islamist-controlled government. Today, the Persecution Project Foundation does amazing work taking care of persecuted and afflicted Christians in the nation of Sudan. Their website address is www.persecutionproject.org

God's Friends Are Passionate About God's Kingdom And The Gospel

CLAAS-UK (Centre for Legal Aid, Assistance and Settlement): This group is unique and also stands out as being one of the few organizations based in the U.K. They have such a profound story, and the work they do for the persecuted Christians in Pakistan, also a nation dear to my heart, is simply incredible. I want you to listen to their story as beautifully told by themselves:

CLAAS-UK (*In their own words*) is a Christian organization committed to addressing ongoing religious persecution in Pakistan, with a particular focus on providing support for persecuted Christians and others from minority religious communities. Since our foundation in 1998, CLAAS staff, including lawyers and volunteers, have championed the cause of persecuted Christians and others, helping thousands of poverty-stricken and traumatized victims of religious persecution.

Our ministry is based on the proclamation of (Proverbs 31:8-9): *"Speak up for those who cannot speak for themselves, for the rights of all who are destitute. Speak up and judge fairly; defend the rights of the poor and needy."* Since 1998, our story has become the story of hundreds of persecuted Christians like Tahir Iqbal, who converted to Christianity and was murdered in jail because of his faith.

Our story is the story of Samuel Masih, who was accused under the Blasphemy law and was killed by the police guard who was supposed to look after him in the hospital. When investigated, the Muslim policeman said that his religious duty to kill a blasphemer was more important than his role as a policeman.

Friend Of God

Our story is the story of hundreds of young girls like Hina, a 14-year-old girl from Sialkot (Punjab), who are being forced into marriages with Muslim men. Or of young women like Chanda from Lahore who are beaten up and abused sexually because of their Christian faith.

Our story is the story of hundreds of families who have been displaced and are living in fear and poverty because a loved one was accused of blasphemy, and the whole family had to leave the village or the town.

Our story is the story of churches that have been burnt up and destroyed, of pastors and priests who have been sent to prison or even killed.

Our story is the story of thousands of friends like you in the U.K., Europe, and other parts of the world who care for the persecuted Christians in Pakistan, who give generously, who pray, and who campaign with us for the abolishment of the unjust blasphemy laws.

Their Mission

CLAAS's mission is to help Christians and the members of other religious minority communities who face persecution in Pakistan. We provide practical support and campaign internationally and locally for the abolishment or revision of unjust laws and policies that are ruining people's lives. Their website is www.claas.org.uk

Epilogue

Friends, as the song says, since God's love got a hold of me, I have been a new creation, and I have truly been forever changed. Someone once beautifully said, "*Wherever a tree was struck by lightning, all its tremulous foliage turned in the direction from which the bolt had come. When the merciful flash of God's great love strikes a heart, then all its tendrils turn to the source of the life-giving light, and we love back again, in sweet reverberation to the primal and original love.*"

I want the love of Christ to penetrate your heart as it did mine. Jesus is who this book is all about. I strongly desire that you be transformed into a new creation in Christ. Do not delay any longer. It is time to surrender your life wholly to the One who is fairer than ten thousand, and His name is Jesus Christ. This is the moment to call on Him, who is the desire of the ages and the centerpiece of civilization.

He wants to make something great out of you. He has a plan and a purpose for you, and I assure you that it is better than you could ever dream of. You may be one who was steadfast but fell away. Well, God is not done with you. It doesn't matter who you have been or what you have done; He still longs to use you today because He loves you. Come home to the father. Come home to Jesus. His arms are open wide. His arm is not short to save you. He is willing, and He is able. So, just say this prayer of salvation with me:

Lord Jesus Christ, I am a weary sinner. Forgive me, Lord. I repent of my sins. Wash me clean with the blood that you shed on the cross for my sake. I promise to forsake all my old ways and I choose to follow you from this day forth. I believe you came to die for me on the cross of Calvary and I confess you as Savior and Lord of my Life. Thank you for your gift of salvation. I declare that I am nothing without you. I accept your promise of salvation, and I declare that I am a born-again child of God. Thank you, Lord.

If you have said that prayer, you are a born-again Christian, and you can certainly now become a friend of God. I welcome you into God's own family. Find a Bible-believing church in your area and get plugged into the community of fellow Christian believers who love Jesus and love others. I would love to hear your testimony and hear how God has changed your life through this book and how the book or our ministry has been a blessing to you. God bless you.

Notes

Chapter 1

1. Wood, W. (2014, August 31). *What Does It Mean To Be "In Love" With God? - Geeks Under Grace.* Geeks under Grace. https://www.geeksundergrace.com/christian-living/what-does-it-mean-to-be-in-love-with-god/

2. Redman, M. (2013). *10,000 Reasons (Bless the Lord)* [Mp3]. SIX STEPS.

3. Hillsong Worship. (2013). *Oceans (Where Feet May Fail)* [Mp3]. HILLSONG.

4. Spurgeon, C. (1887, May 8). *The Friend of God.*

Chapter 2

1. Maclaren, A. (1932). *Expositions of Holy scripture / [Vol. 15], Second Timothy, Titus, Philemon and Hebrews, Hebrews, chaps. VII to end, Epistle of James.* Doran, [Ca.

Chapter 3

1. Bridges, C. (1977). *A commentary on Proverbs.* Banner of Truth Trust, Printing.

2. "The beauties of the late Right Hon. Edmund Burke, selected from the writings, &c. of that extraordinary man, ... To which is prefixed, a sketch of the life, with some original anecdotes of Mr. Burke. In two volumes.: [pt.1]." In the digital collection Eighteenth Century Collections Online. https://name.umdl.umich.edu/004795912.0001.001.

University of Michigan Library Digital Collections. Accessed August 22, 2024.

3. Austin, D. (2015). *The American Preacher, Or, a Collection of Sermons from Some of the Most Eminent Preachers, Now Living in the United States.* Palala Press. JOHN WITHERSPOON.

4. Sovereign Grace Music, & Altrogge, M. (1986). *I Stand in Awe of You.* Sovereign Grace Praise (BMI).

5. Bridges, J. (2016). *The Practice of Godliness* (p. 29). NavPress.

6. Jeshurun, M. (2021, September 6). *THE "FEAR OF THE LORD" OUR GREATEST TREASURE.* Wordpress.com; WordPress.com. https://michaeljeshurun.wordpress.com/2021/09/06/the-fear-of-the-lord-our-greatest-treasure/. Thomas Watson.

7. Maclaren, A. (1932). *Expositions of Holy scripture / [Vol. 15], Second Timothy, Titus, Philemon and Hebrews, Hebrews, chaps. VII to end, Epistle of James.* Doran, [Ca.

8. Watson, T. (1600). *Thomas Watson: Ten Commandments - Christian Classics Ethereal Library.* Ccel.org. https://ccel.org/ccel/watson/commandments/commandments.toc.html

9. Bevere, J. (2010). *The Fear Of The Lord* (p. 2). Charisma Media.

Notes

Chapter 4

1. Houghton, I. (2005). *He knows my name* [Mp3]. Integrity Media.

Chapter 5

1. Hillsong Worship. (1994, February 27). *People Just Like Us* [Mp3]. Hillsong, Geoff Bullock, Russell Fragar and Darlene Zschech.

2. Brooks, T. (1655). *Smooth Stones Taken from Ancient Brooks.* Gracegems.org. https://www.gracegems.org/Brooks/smooth_stones_Brooks.htm

3. McGee, J. Vernon. (2014). *The Fellowship of Believers - Thru the Bible with Dr. J. Vernon McGee.* Oneplace.com. https://www.oneplace.com/ministries/thru-the-bible-with-j-vernon-mcgee/read/articles/fellowship-of-believers-9838.html

Chapter 6

1. Maclaren, A. (1932). *Expositions of Holy scripture / [Vol. 15], Second Timothy, Titus, Philemon and Hebrews, Hebrews, chaps. VII to end, Epistle of James.* Doran, [Ca.

2. Edwards, J. (2018). *Quotes Jonathan Edwards | FaithWriters.* Faithwriters.com. https://www.faithwriters.com/article-details.php?id=196225

Friend Of God

Chapter 7

1. Moody, D. L. (2023, May 18). *Christian Quotes by D.L. Moody - 316 Quotes.* 316 Quotes. https://316quotes.com/d-l-moody/

2. Punchard, E. G., & Ellicott, C. J. (1870). *The General Epistle of James.* Cassell And Co.

3. Barnes, A. (1849). *Notes, Explanatory and Practical, on the General Epistles of James, Peter, John and Jude.* Albert Barnes.

Chapter 8

1. Miles, C. A. (1912). *In the Garden.* Charles Austin Miles.

2. Leonard Ravenhill. (2010). *>From the Heart of Leonard Ravenhill.* Grace Fellowship Manchester. https://gfmanchester.com/from-the-heart-of-leonard-ravenhill

3. Cymbala, J. (2023, January 25). *Pastor Jim Cymbala and the Necessity of Prayer - Bible Apologetics - A DAILY DEVOTIONAL.* Bible Apologetics - a DAILY DEVOTIONAL. https://bibleapologetics.org/pastor-jim-cymbala-and-the-necessity-of-prayer/

4. Staten, K. (1996, January 1). *Lord I Thirst for You* [Mp3]. Integrity Media.

5. Hillsong Worship. (2001, February 25). *To You* [Mp3]. Hillsong.

6. Anonymous

Notes

7. Howgill, F. (2024). *Francis Howgill Quote*. A-Z Quotes. https://www.azquotes.com/quote/837719

8. Jones, E. S. (2024). *E. Stanley Jones Quote: "To talk with God, no breath is lost. Talk on! To walk with God, no strength is lost. Walk on! To wait on God, no time is..."* Quotefancy.com. https://quotefancy.com/quote/1261089/E-Stanley-Jones-To-talk-with-God-no-breath-is-lost-Talk-on-To-walk-with-God-no-strength

Chapter 9

1. A W Tozer. (2013). *The Pursuit of God*. Stori Imprint. (Original work published 1948)

2. MacLaren, A. (1897). *Music for the soul : daily readings for a year from the writings of Rev. Alexander MacLaren*. A.C. Armstrong and Son.

3. Smith, M., & Barnett, M. (2000, December 1). *Breathe - this is the air I breathe* [Mp3]. Reunion Records Inc.

4. AW TOZER. (n.d.). *20 Timeless Worship Quotes by A.W. Tozer | Renewing Worship*. Renewing Worship. https://www.renewingworshipnc.org/quotes-by-tozer/

5. Fosdick, H. E. (2024). *Harry Emerson Fosdick Quote*. A-Z Quotes. https://www.azquotes.com/quote/99919

Chapter 10

1. Saint Teresa . (n.d.). *Saint Teresa of Avila Quotes*. BrainyQuote. https://www.brainyquote.com/quotes/saint_teresa_of_avila_209866

Chapter 11

1. Charles Spurgeon. (2012, March 21). *Quotes: Dying to Self*. Revlisad.com; Revlisad.com. https://revlisad.com/2012/03/21/quotes-dying-to-self/

2. Brainerd, D. (2024). *David Brainerd Quote*. A-Z Quotes. https://www.azquotes.com/quote/715695

3. Tozer, A. W. (2007). *The Best of A. W. Tozer Book Two* (p. 149). Moody Publishers. (Original work published 1948)

4. St. Ignatius of Loyola. (2011, October 25). *Daily Quote from St. Ignatius of Loyola*. Integrated Catholic Life™. https://integratedcatholiclife.org/2011/10/daily-quote-from-st-ignatius-of-loyola-12/

5. Paul David Tripp. (2013). *Dangerous Calling*. Carina Press.

Chapter 13

1. Maclaren, A. (1932). *Expositions of Holy scripture / [Vol. 15], Second Timothy, Titus, Philemon and Hebrews, Hebrews, chaps. VII to end, Epistle of James*. Doran, [Ca.

Notes

Chapter 14

1. Bridges, J. (2014). *The Pursuit of Holiness.* Tyndale House.

2. Chambers, O. (2010). *My Utmost for His Highest.* Our Daily Bread Publishing.

3. Walden, K. (2019, August 24). *Robert Cawdray - Daily Christian Quotes.* Daily Christian Quotes. https://www.dailychristianquote.com/robert-cawdray-2/

4. Zschech, D. (2023). *Every time you open up your heart in obedience to God and worship Him with all your heart, all your mind, and all your soul, our beautiful Lord responds with His magnificent presence. - The Behaviour University.* The Behaviour University. https://quotes.behaviour-university.com/quote/2173275/

5. St. Augustine, & Pusey, E. B. (1951). *The confessions of St. Augustine, Bishop of Hippo.* Dutton.

Chapter 15

1. Spurgeon, C. (1863, April 5). *Death and life in Christ* [Sermon]. Sunday Service.

About The Author

Stony Kalango is an inspirational author, Bible teacher, and minister of the gospel. As an evangelist, Stony is committed to the expansion of God's kingdom on this earth.

Born in Nigeria, Stony had the call of God on his life at a very young age, and preached his first sermon at the age of eight. He started ministry by preaching with a hand megaphone on streets early in the mornings with his parents. God's hand has been on his life ever since.

He held his first gospel crusade – Evening of Hope at age 16. Now Stony has carried on that vision through evangelistic meetings like Nights of Hope that are held around the world as he seeks to reach many with the amazing gospel of Jesus Christ. Stony has been blessed to be a guest on TV and radio stations around the nation and is credentialed with the Assemblies of God.

Notes

He is passionate about persecuted Christians around the world and is also an avid soccer fan. In his free time, he enjoys practicing his sword skills, playing soccer and watching historical war and medieval movies.

He is married to Olivia Kalango and they have two beautiful daughters, Honor and Hadassah. They currently reside in Oklahoma City and serve at their home church, Revive Church, Edmond Oklahoma.

Stony would love to connect with you so please free to reach out to the ministry at any time and connect with us on social media. For speaking engagements and to learn more about Stony and his ministry, please visit us on our website - **stonykalango.com**.

Stay Connected

Facebook.com/stonykalangoministries

Youtube.com/@stonykalangoministries

Instagram.com/stonykalango

X.com/stonykalango

Other Books

Pencil Sharp: 7 Key Lessons From A Pencil To Becoming The Best That You Can Be.

You Can You Will You Must: Break the Shackle of Mediocrity, Overcome Life's Obstacles, Achieve Greatness.

Note: For bulk orders of Stony's books, please reach out to us at info@stonykalango.com.

Made in the USA
Columbia, SC
20 September 2024

9f91b521-4abb-4c60-a60e-0f8e3a097f04R01